Feminist Narratives and the
Sociology of Religion

Feminist Narratives and the Sociology of Religion

EDITED BY
NANCY NASON-CLARK
MARY JO NEITZ

ALTAMIRA
PRESS

A Division of
ROWMAN & LITTLEFIELD PUBLISHERS, INC.
Walnut Creek • Lanham • New York • Oxford

ALTAMIRA PRESS
A Division of Rowman & Littlefield Publishers, Inc.
1630 North Main Street, #367
Walnut Creek, CA 94596
www.altamirapress.com

Rowman & Littlefield Publishers, Inc.
4720 Boston Way
Lanham, MD 20706

12 Hid's Copse Road
Cumnor Hill, Oxford OX2 9JJ, England

British Library Cataloguing in Publication Information Available

Library of Congress Cataloging-in-Publication Data
Feminist narratives and the sociology of religion / [edited by] Nancy Nason-Clark, Mary
Jo Nietz.
    p. cm.
  Includes bibliographical references.
  ISBN 0-7591-0197-3 (alk. paper) — ISBN 0-7591-0198-1 (pbk.: alk. paper)
   1. Religion and sociology. 2. Feminism—Religious aspects. I. Nason-Clark, Nancy,
1956- II. Neitz, Mary Jo, 1951-

BL60 .F46 2001
306.6'082—dc21

                                     2001046343

Printed in the United States of America

Contents

Preface

Like most books, this one has a story within a story. It came together as a result of several factors: Nancy was elected as President of the Association for the Sociology of Religion (ASR) and she selected Mary Jo Neitz to offer the Paul Hanly Furfey Lecture at the 1999 annual meetings, where her presidential address would be delivered. The traditional custom in the Association for the Sociology of Religion is that these two invited addresses appear in print in the Society's journal, *Sociology of Religion*, a short time after they have been delivered. The editor of the journal at that time, Joe Tamney, invited Nancy to serve as guest editor for a special issue of the journal, the one in which her presidential address would appear. She invited Mary Jo to collaborate on that venture. Together we invited a number of established women sociologists and graduate students who research issues related to gender and religion to participate in the special issue, and in so doing, to complement our invited addresses. These essays and research notes were first published as volume 61, number 4, of *Sociology of Religion*, in December 2000. Erik Hanson of AltaMira Press was the efficient midwife responsible for bringing to life the book version of our essays, and we acknowledge his role with thanks. Bill Swatos, executive officer of the ASR, offered advice and encouragement. Barbara Fisher Townsend, our editorial assistant, always goes well beyond the call of duty and though we have come to expect her diligence, we hope never to take it for granted.

Feminist Narratives and the Sociology of Religion is a collection of essays that seek to cultivate the growing gender and feminist consciousness in our area of study and to challenge us — established scholars and graduate students alike — to be cognizant of the location from which we write. The narratives contained in our edited collection reveal the interplay between biography and scholarly pursuits, the relationship between academic rigor, personal passion and life story. We trust that the volume will open new doors for dialog at professional meetings and in print. This volume captures a particular moment in an emerging dialog. We look forward to the inclusion of new viewpoints and changing points of departure as the dialog continues. While we recognize that there are many competing voices in the academy, we hope you will be refreshed and challenged by the plethora of feminist voices assembled in our book.

Nancy Nason-Clark and Mary Jo Neitz

1

Feminist Narratives and the Sociology of Religion

Nancy Nason-Clark
Mary Jo Neitz

In working on this volume we as editors confirmed what we had suspected for some time: despite a number of differences in our graduate training, professional work experience, and geographical location, we both shared what might be called a generational experience. We are part of a particular cohort of women who became feminists and sociologists at the same point in our lives, and saw these activities as being inextricably tied together. In our careers as university professors we have sought to bring our feminism to the academy, and our research to religious organizations, institutions, and individuals in ways that had the potential to make a difference in the lives of ordinary women and men. Our desire to do sociological research that puts women, their lives and their experiences — as well as issues of gender — at the center of any sociological analysis was shaped by our participation in the women's movement. This was the context from which we began — and continue — to ask questions within the sociology of religion. Editing this volume has given us the opportunity to further examine the connections between what we study and how we study it, not only in our own lives, but in the lives of other scholars who are researching various aspects of religious phenomena and gender.

NARRATIVES OF LIFE AND WORK

We have invited a number of women sociologists who identify as feminists and who devote a central place in their research to the intersection of gender and religion to join us in reflecting on feminist perspectives and research in the sociology of religion. We asked them for narratives relating how they came to study this intersection, and the connections between their academic work and their non-academic lives. Brainstorming together, we came up with a list of questions which we posed to the contributors:

- What did you start out intending to address in your research?
- What are some of the lessons that you have learned along the way?

1

- At what point did your research begin to take on a life of its own?
- What are the social action implications of your research or its findings?
- Has your work challenged any of the taken-for-granted notions of scholarship in the sociology of religion? If so, how?
- In what ways has it contributed to theoretical or methodological debates in our field?
- Have you come to reconsider boundaries between the sacred and the secular?
- Has there been any passionate resistance to your work, its findings or implications? And, what is next on your research agenda?

In essence, we wanted to know about the trajectory along which their lives and work had taken them as scholars in the sociology of religion.

In focusing on feminist paths, and in weaving the connections between our lives and our work, we are part of a large shift in the academic disciplines occasioned by the explosion of scholarship about women.[1] One indicator of this broader movement is the fact that the Sex and Gender section is the largest section in the American Sociological Association. Another indicator is the recent publication of edited books in which scholars in this path-breaking generation reflect on their experiences as feminists and sociologists.[2] Looking back over the growth in feminist research in sociology, we note religion was not high on the priority list of issues to be examined by feminist sociologists. While sociology journals published a spate of special issues on scholarship devoted to women and gender issues in the 1970s , it was two decades later before an issue devoted to gender and religion was published in the *Sociology of Religion*.[3] In her essay for this volume, Joy Charlton describes going to the SSSR/RRA meetings in 1978 when the theme of the meeting was "Religion and Sex Roles: Challenge and Change." Indicating how times have changed, she notes that, at those meetings, there were no papers on clergy women, but three on women in seminary, one of which was the research she was presenting from her own MA thesis. In the early 1990s one of us was asked to write a review essay about feminist research in the sociology of religion: with the exception of Ruth Wallace's presidential address for ASR in 1975, and an article by Marie Augusta Neal (1979),

---

[1] For an early account looking across several disciplines see *Feminist scholarship: Kindling in the groves of academia* by Dubois, Kelly, Kennedy, Korsmeyer and Robinson (1985). Stacey and Thorne addressed particular conditions in sociology in their article, *"The missing revolution in feminist sociology."* For a recent assessment providing an overview of theoretical questions now guiding work on gender in sociology see *Revisioning gender* (1999) edited by M. M. Ferree, J. Lorber, and B. Hess.

[2] For two such volumes focusing on sociologists see Orlans and Wallace (1994) and Laslett and Thorne (1997).

[3] For example, Joan Huber edited a special issue of the *Journal of American Sociology* in 1973. In 1993, following the Ed Lehman ASR presidency, and publishing his presidential address (Lehman 1993), *Sociology of Religion* published a thematic issue devoted to "Religion and Gender Relationships." Prior to that, in 1987, the journal published a set of four articles under the heading of "Recent Research on Feminism and Religion."

there are few examples of feminist work published in the field before the 1980s (Neitz 1993).

This book is in part a reflection on the work of a generation of scholars. We want to celebrate the establishment of the subfield of gender and religion, a subfield which did not exist when this generation was in graduate school. We also take this as an opportunity to think not just about where we have been, but also where we are going. We want to consider what was left unexamined in the first twenty years of feminist scholarship in our field, and to think about what needs consideration now. This set of essays from established women academics, both individually and as a group, gives us insight into how location matters, and how knowledge is situated in particular contexts.

As part of the process of editing this volume, we asked two senior scholars for input: Nancy Ammerman and Helen Rose Ebaugh. In their comments to us as editors, both reviewers noted the recurrent theme of narrative construction and the interplay and mutual impact of biographies and research agendas. We want to note our appreciation of their "invisible work" on this volume: it helped us (and the authors) clarify and strengthen the connections between the pieces. In her review, Ammerman writes that the chapters put forward "the theme of narrative construction and the way women's lives, full as they are of disruptions and contradictions, illuminate and are illuminated by that process." Ebaugh notes the close link between researcher, researched, and method of study. In the chapters to follow several additional themes are highlighted, including the role of mentorship, and the presence or absence of barriers to full partnership in the research process. As well, all the essays talk of silence, hiddenness, and how we make heard the credibility of the people whose lives we have chosen to study. Not only does listening to new voices alert us to the complexity of issues, but often as researchers, we are changed in the process. Charlton, Davidman, and Jacobs examine directly the challenges women face in constructing religious, work, and other narratives. Lummis and Nesbitt challenge the notion that there is a single definition of feminism or feminist research. Foltz's essay is especially helpful in drawing our attention to the location of the researcher, and Becker shows us how a younger generation of women scholars are adapting feminist theory and feminist methods as they strive to understand the social world with a "third wave" feminist lens.

REPORTS FROM THE FIELD

While self-reflection is useful, it can only partly accomplish our task. We wanted another perspective. Although they are just beginning to chart career trajectories, we wanted to hear what questions younger scholars were choosing to work on, and how issues of religion and gender touch them as they begin their research agendas.

Within the women's movement there is an increasing consciousness about feminist generations: those who became feminists in the late sixties and early seventies had a conversion experience, whereas those who became feminists in the late 1980s and 1990s came into a world in which feminism was certainly present. They learned about feminism from women they knew, often from their own mothers or from teachers. Even in a context of backlash against feminism, those who became feminists in the eighties and nineties report also having received feminist "nurturance." These feminists came into a world that was quite different from the world encountered by those who had come before. It was a world changed substantially, partly due to the efforts of second wave feminists. The "third wave feminists" have brought their own questions and concerns to the women's movement; based in their own life experiences they have offered new frames for the movement, frames which extended challenges to the earlier feminists as well as to the world outside.[4]

In the work of the current generation of graduate students we see a similar process: some of the things we struggled to establish are now taken for granted, new questions come to light, and new challenges arise to both mainstream study and the work of feminist foremothers. We see continuities and discontinuities with the work of our generation. In an effort to bring some of these to the fore, we asked a number of graduate students currently working on religion and gender to write "reports from the field." Our thinking was that they would share with us what they are learning: we want to see how they are learning it, who their questions are being shaped by, and how they see themselves challenging the prevailing wisdom, including feminist wisdom.

Heyer-Gray brings questions about the gendered nature of religious work as performed by those outside the clergy. Detwiler Breidenbach examines the intersection of gender and race in a community of Mexican immigrants. Albee's research dialog with a second-generation woman pastor portrays the interplay of agency and structures, only one of which is gender. Spencer-Arsenault considers the ritualized awe surrounding the role of the Virgin Mary, while Sleep extracts some "nuggets" from her fieldwork amongst Pentecostal families. These scholars use feminist perspectives in different ways, both building on and challenging "blind spots" in the work of earlier feminists. The established scholars and the students exemplify a dynamic feminism, alive and well in the sociology of religion.

Like any edited collection, neither the list of established scholars, nor the students invited to participate, are exhaustive of those in our field. By design, we see this book as inviting more dialog, more reflective pieces, more perspectives than what could be reported in these pages alone. Our goal is to cultivate the growing feminist and gender consciousness in our midst and to challenge us —

---

[4] For an analysis of feminist generations see Whittier (1995); for a discussion of feminist nurturance see Downing (1992); for examples of third wave feminism see Walker (1995).

established scholars and graduate students alike — to be cognizant of the location from which we write. We celebrate the opportunities we have for learning from each other as colleagues, and as students and mentors, while acknowledging how these relationships are shaped by the institutional contexts in which we work, and our own relative positions in those institutions. There are important issues not discussed fully in this volume: issues of funding, of feminist methodology, of field ethics, of structural barriers to pursuing one's life work, and how gender intersects with other structures of oppression. May those (ongoing) conversations continue to occur at our conferences and later in print. We trust you will both enjoy and be challenged by the plethora of feminist voices assembled in this volume.

REFERENCES

Downing, J. 1992. Identities and social movements: Becoming feminists, 1968-1992. MA Thesis: University of Missouri.

Dubois, E., G. P. Kelly, E. L. Kennedy, C. Korsmeyer, and L. Robinson. 1985. *Feminist scholarship: Kindling in the groves of Academia*. Urbana: University of Illinois Press.

Ferree, M., J. Lorber, B. B. Hess, and M. Marx. 1999. *Revisioning gender*. Thousand Oaks, CA: Sage Publishing.

Laslett, B., and B. Thorne. 1997. *Feminist sociology: Life histories of a movement*. New Brunswick, NJ: Rutgers University Press.

Lehman, E. 1993. Gender and ministry style: Things not what they seem. *Sociology of Religion* 54:1-11.

Neal, M. A. 1979. Women in religious symbolism and organization. *Sociological Inquiry* 45:33-39.

Neitz, M.J. 1993. Inequality and difference: Feminist research in the sociology of religion. In *Future for Religion? New Paradigms for Social Analysis*, edited by W. H. Swatos, pp. 165-84. Thousand Oaks, CA: Sage.

Orlans, K., and R. Wallace. 1994. Gender and the academic experience: *Berkeley Women Sociologists*. Lincoln: University of Nebraska Press.

Stacey J., and B. Thorne. 1985. The missing feminist revolution in sociology. *Social Problems* 32:301-16.

Walker, R. 1995. *To be real: Telling the truth and changing the face of feminism*. New York: Anchor Books.

Wallace, R. 1975. Bringing women in. *Sociological Analysis* 36:291-303.

Whittier, N. 1995. *Feminist generations: The persistence of the radical women's movement*. Philadelphia, PA: Temple University Press.

2

Making the Sacred Safe: Woman Abuse and Communities of Faith

Nancy Nason-Clark
University of New Brunswick

I am assuming that this is a safe place to tell a few stories, mostly taken from my personal life narrative, illustrating what I believe are some of the challenges ahead for us as social science professionals, illustrating the complexity, or multiple layers of reality, in our research programs, and hopefully inspiring us to take up the challenge of scholarship into the next century. I plan to use the metaphor of a journey where there are road signs, blinders, and blindspots impairing our vision, travelling companions, and a navigational route we plan to follow. Once I have introduced us to these mental images, I will explore how these have impacted upon my research on woman abuse in faith communities.[1]

A few years ago now, our family attended the annual barbeque that is organized by the graduate students of the Psychology Department at the University of New Brunswick, to celebrate the beginning of a new academic year. The event was being hosted by one of David's (my husband) faculty colleagues who lives in a rather remote location in the countryside, a place where he can think in solace about animal physiology and maintain his ongoing love of

---

[1] The Religion and Violence Research Team was established in 1992 by Nancy Nason-Clark and she has coordinated it since its inception. Its membership includes both academic researchers and denominational partners working in collaboration; Rev. Terry Atkinson, Dr. Lori Beaman, Dr. Lois Mitchell, Ms. Christy Terris Hoyt, Rev. Sheila McCrea are team members and Amanda Henry Steeves, Michelle Spencer-Arsenault, and Lisa Hanson have served as graduate research assistants. Projects have included the Atlantic District of the Wesleyan Church, the United Baptist Convention of the Atlantic Provinces, the Maritime Conference of the United Church, the Anglican Church (Province of New Brunswick), and the Maritime Division of the Salvation Army.

Financial support of our research initiative and community consultations has been provided by the Louisville Institute for the Study of Protestantism and American Culture, the Social Sciences and Humanities Research Council of Canada, the Department of the Solicitor General, Secretary of State Canada, Status of Women Canada, the Lawson Foundation, the Constant Jacquet Award of the Religious Research Association, the Fichter Fund of the Association of the Sociology of Religion, the Muriel McQueen Centre for Family Violence Research, and the University of New Brunswick Research Fund. Financial and in-kind contributions have also been provided by the participating denominations.

sheep farming. As we got closer to our final destination, but further from civilization, there were home-made signposts: the Greek sign for psi led the way. The gathering had the usual beverages, food, and entertainment. We ate, we played volleyball, we talked 'til our children were weary, and then we went home. So far so good: a rather innocuous gathering of professors, graduate students, partners, offspring, and sheep. But, there was an interesting development.

The next evening whilst we were eating dinner, the phone rang. It was a young woman in one of David's undergraduate classes, who attended a very conservative church in town. With some degree of panic in her voice, she wanted to "share" information about a particular professor who was "a known Satan worshipper." Undeterred by David's response to her accusation, she claimed that a ritual event had occurred at his home only the day before. "Something must be done," she protested. "There were sacrifices and sex. . . ." Before she could finish, David exclaimed, "We were there, it was a barbeque, our children played games on the lawn. You are very mistaken. Rest assured it was a very innocent gathering. Perhaps too much food, or too much boasting. That's all." Once he was off the phone, David grumbled about the fact that the student did not recognize the psi sign for what it was, a make-shift marker for a psychology party, where the Greek symbol would be clearly recognized by all would-be attenders. It was not a pitchfork, marking the way to a ritual event.

But the story does not end here. Local people in this remote part of our Canadian province, like the psychology student, misinterpreted the sign. The professor received death threats, his children were harassed at school, truckloads of youth would pull up into his yard, look around, and squeal their tires, he was visited by the police and the Fire Marshall several times to warn him of impending danger: apparently a vigilante group has been formed to burn his home and force him from the community. Local and national papers ran the story. A tempest in a teapot created by misinterpreting the road signs.

There is an important lesson for us in this story. As sociologists of religion, we can sometimes read the road signs — see them clearly, but interpret them falsely. From one perspective — that of the locals — the signs pointed to potential danger. They had an intuitive logic about them for they explained what might seem rather unexplainable: why a rather affluent, educated man would choose to live in such an isolated area cut off from the sights and sounds of the university and government town by his own desire to be set apart rather than by economic or intellectual exclusion. But from his perspective, the hobby farm in a remote, rural context was an oasis, not a prison.

You and I may not choose to live on a hobby farm, but I suspect most of us would defend his right to do so, even in the face of encroaching university politics and management models that define university professors as sheep in need of a CEO shepherd. We need to be careful how we interpret the sign-posts. Religion is not dying, the spiritual quest is very much alive, but there are new players on the scene: the hegemonic powerful clerical elite has been challenged, but the search for meaning, identity, and the celebration of life through ritual and song continues. Secularizing and sacralizing forces co-exist, confounding how we sometimes read the sign-posts. As embodied gendered spirits (McGuire 1990), women and men shape their experiences, their beliefs, as well as their daily practices (Ammerman 1997), even as they have been shaped by social, economic, political, and structural forces outside of direct individual or collective control. Reading the signposts accurately and interpreting them correctly has been an ongoing learning experience for me as I have studied wife abuse over the last eight years.

That brings me to the second point I want to raise about academic societies and hence about us. As social scientists, our professional task is not necessarily to defend religious narratives, but to document their power and impact, as well as to defend the individual freedom to pursue them. In this role, we need to be careful not to dismiss the power of "isms" in our own lives and thinking. In illustrating this point, I am reminded of an episode of Archie Bunker; the forty-plusers in the audience today will remember the series, no doubt. Well, in this episode, Archie and his ever-nervous wife, Edith, were having a theological debate. Back and forth it went. As Edith gained moral ground, Archie grew angry. Finally, sensing that he was losing the debate, he exclaimed to his wife. "Edith, God don't want to be defended by no dingbat!"

Like a horse at a race, we can have professional blinders on our eyes, limiting our explorations and our explanations to a particular ideological comfort zone. Sometimes, scholars can be so narrowed by their training, their prejudices, and their preferences, that not only do they limit their own thinking, but they create walls and barriers for their students and their colleagues. As Penny Becker and Nancy Eiesland (1997) have shown in their recent edited collection, there is more than one way to ask questions, more than one story to tell.

My point is rather simple: sometimes we can extricate the splinter in the eye of a participant in our research agenda, though we cannot recognize a piece of timber in our own. Dingbats or not, we cling to ideological positions that stand on very shaky empirical grounds. We are unwilling or unable to realize that the forces that shape our own thinking and structural realities, including those of contemporary academia, religious institutions, or our personal life narratives place blinders on our research eyes or harbour blind spots in our analysis. Negotiating the delicate terrain of our own social, religious, ethnic, and gendered experience, coupled with our training, past research endeavours and ongoing social scientific preferences, makes understanding some of us almost as interesting as the data and theory that we expound.

At the 1998 SSSR meetings, I had been invited to give a paper on how my research on wife abuse had impacted on my own life. Entitled, *From the heart of my laptop*, I explored how my life and thinking had been altered as a result of researching violence (Nason-Clark 2001b). I am not a victim of violence myself, but my social location as researcher and developing role as activist continues to have a major impact on me. I am not the same person I was before I started researching wife abuse: I hope I have become a more caring person, more committed to social change, more impatient with inequitable social structures, more convinced of the comfortable location from which I speak.

So, we need to be careful how we interpret the road signs, be careful of blinders and blind spots, and then thirdly, we need to open up the feast to newcomers, or journey with some new travelling companions. If our professional association is a closed club, I want to find the exit door. Graduate students and junior scholars add immeasurably to our collective wisdom, enrich the questions we ask and the responses we receive. Whether we are in the field, in the lab, or in the library, ongoing stretching of our minds and of our paradigms is a critical component to sociological inquiry. Challenging taken-for-granted wisdom, sometimes by pushing the envelope of proponents, is what professional meetings need to foster. On this point, I am distressed by the low attendance at many sessions, and the relative ease by which one could enter and leave academic meetings without being engaged in a scholarly dialogue with anyone. I think we have become more inclusive as of late, but let me again illustrate this point by a short story from my own life.

In 1980, at the age of 23, I came to my first ASR meeting to present a paper based on my completed MA thesis. For me, there were three notable things that happened at those meetings: 1) It was hard to find a community of women scholars with whom to dialogue, because there were so few women in attendance and because there were no networking venues; 2) besides my MA thesis supervisor, Kenneth Westhues, who has always been a stalwart supporter of his students, no one engaged me in any dialogue about my paper or my scholarly interests, though I must admit there seemed to be undue attention to my personal life; and 3) at one of the plenary social events, an older professor suggested I direct my Ph.D. thesis to matters other than religion, or perhaps, redirect my talent to a career other than the academy, because in his words, "I would never get a job." Let me be very blunt here: as faculty and as members of the ASR professional association, how do we ever expect to become more visible in the discipline and rejuvenate our conversations and debates if we scare good students away? Each generation brings new questions, new perspectives, and new challenges to the social scientific study of religion. We need to be on our guard against any form of intellectual elitism which suggests that the king's table is full, that there is nothing new to be learned. Welcoming new scholars, integrating students and making space for diverse and often contradictory points of view should, *must*, characterize academic societies and our journal. Smaller organizations have the flexibility to adapt and to respond to changing times, as the history of the ASR reveals we have done. We all need to be committed to continuing that tradition.

Integrating diversity is something that the multi-disciplinary team approach has taught me over the last five years. When I was first approached by The

Muriel McQueen Fergusson Foundation about developing a national center, I was overwhelmed with the size of the task and my own personal and professional limitations. But working together with several other academic women, developing a model for research and then personal strategies to achieve it, have strengthened my resolve that social change and institutional change is possible when shared vision is present. To be sure, there are challenges to having many cooks in the kitchen, but the quality of the cuisine is worth the effort. New networks of scholars, different constellations of researchers, weaving levels of experience and occupational location—these are contemporary themes that would enrich our journey as well.

My fourth preliminary point is this: we need to think very carefully about the link between the ivory tower and the community that we serve, or where the journey is taking us. Another point, another story. Many years ago when I was studying in England, I had occasion to interview an evangelical minister and his wife who lived just outside one of the major industrial cities in that country. The appointment was set for early evening and I remember well walking briskly to their home from the train station, feeling a little uneasy about the approaching darkness and the ominous, but still intermittent, drops of rain. The interview, which lasted about an hour, gave us an opportunity to talk about forms of ministry open to women and men in the church. The time came for me to leave. As I was about to walk through the door into the darkness of the night, the pastor called me back. "I am really concerned about your safety walking to the train station at this hour." His wife agreed, noting that the gentle rain had matured into a "down-pour." I stepped back into their hallway, thankful that they had been responsive to the conditions outside. "We want to pray that God would keep you safe and dry," the pastor said rather softly. They prayed and I left. As I walked past their car in the driveway, I thought about how this couple might have enabled their prayer to be answered immediately by driving me back to the station. How could these spiritual leaders be so insensitive? Rather than praying for my safety, why didn't they get their car keys? But I am thankful that they didn't, for in many different contexts in my professional life I am reminded of the irony of the story I have just told. Do we care about the people whose lives we seek to understand and explain? What level of responsibility do you and I have — situated as most of us are in the ivory tower — to the communities where we live, the students whom we teach, and the institutions that pay for our bread and butter? Contentious though it be, I want to suggest that with knowledge comes social responsibility: Scholarship devoid of social activism is like a car that is never driven for fear of an accident, a house too clean for guests, a restaurant preparing for service but never finalizing its menu, a church so busy with programs that it cannot help hurting men and women.

Now I can hear the objections already, those voices from the chalk-filled lecture halls of my past (I always sat near the front) or the cyberspace of my present. The voices believe in the separation not only of church and state, but the separation of the university from the community at large. The ivory tower has changed, the moat has been removed, the doors are open, and many people heretofore prevented from walking its hallowed halls are crossing the draw-bridge, with their questions, with their life experiences, and sometimes with their anger. From my professional vantage point, boundaries are being eroded all around: in our disciplines, as inter-disciplinary and cross-disciplinary studies challenge us to think outside the boxes where we have grown comfortable; in our research, as funding bodies have embraced multi-disciplinary teams to respond to questions that single disciplines alone seem impotent to understand; in our universities, as governments have challenged us to think about issues of relevance, cost-effectiveness, and the training and intellectual needs of our students; and in religious bodies, where the boundaries are, in the words of Hoge, Johnson and Luidens (1994), vanishing. Boundaries, borders, and bridges are all themes of recent ASR presidential addresses (Ammerman 1997; Warner 1997; Roof 1998). Why? Because they tell us something very important about the social structures and social processes surrounding the study of religion in contemporary culture. Our day presents some unique opportunities, to offer what Stevens-Arroyo (1998) calls "user-friendly sociology," or to disseminate our findings where they have the potential to be read by non-specialists, as Carl Dudley (1999) reminded us recently.

There are a number of recent examples of how this is being operationalized in our midst. I have chosen two areas as examples: multiculturalism and women clergy. Responding to the changing landscape of religious multiculturalism as Steve Warner (Warner and Wittner 1998) and Helen Rose Ebaugh (Ebaugh and Chafetz 2000, 1999) are doing with separate teams and diverse questions, or responding to the feminist challenge to clerical power as Adair Lummis (Winter, Lummis, and Stokes 1994), Paula Nesbitt (1997), Mark Chaves (1997), Ed Lehman (1993), and others have done. Whether the puzzle has ethnic or gender overtones, our task is to unravel some of the riddles in religious life and religious expression (c.f., Kraybill 1988; Davidman 1991; Townsend Gilkes 1996; Kaufman 1991; Peña 1995) and to do it in a way that neither detracts from scholarship nor fears entering the marketplace, as Eileen Barker has shown by example (Barker 1995). I must admit, or confess, that what brings the most satisfaction to my professional life these days is thinking together with others outside the academy of the implications of our research.

The metaphor of a journey, the signposts, the potential blind spots, the journey companions, and deciding which road to follow offers a scant intro-duction to my program of research, and the topic to which we will now turn. *Making the sacred safe*, my title, is meant to reflect the social action implications of explicating someone's story. And the story I have been attempting to tell revolves around what happens when an abused religious woman looks to her faith community for help. It is a multi-faceted story and I want to tell it today, briefly, from six different perspectives.

WOMAN ABUSE AND FAITH COMMUNITIES

The Story from the Scholarly and Feminist Literature

Wife abuse is an age-old issue, but talking about it in the public square is rather new. As a culture, we have become aware of the prevalence and severity of violence in the family context through two main sources: family researchers, and feminist activists. Over the last twenty-five years, psychologists, sociologists, and social workers investigating family life have begun to document its darker side: child abuse, wife abuse, couple violence, and elder abuse (Strauss, Gelles, and Steinmetz 1980; DeKeseredy and McLeod 1998). Employing diverse methodologies, from national surveys to clinical case study data, they began to reveal the frequency and severity of abusive acts between family members and sexual intimates (Straus and Gelles 1986; Feld and Straus 1989; Statistics Canada 1993; Martin 1981).

But the story met with opposition. Even in the academy, there was resistance to the message. Family life was basically good, went the theory particularly forcefully espoused by functionalism, it was good for men, good for women, and good for children. If such abusive acts occurred, they were rare and characteristic of families or individuals deprived of the social capital required for peaceful co-existence in our contemporary Western culture.

Yet, concern for children began to tug on America's heart and on her apron-strings. Children were vulnerable and could not easily be blamed for choosing their parents poorly. As a consequence, the Western world began to respond in emotion and in dollars to the suffering of toddlers, school children, and teens (Bross, Krugman, Lenherr, Rosenberg, Schmitt 1988).

The story of wife abuse took a slightly different turn in the road. In the 1960s, the second wave of feminism began to sweep North America, strengthening in the decades to immediately follow (G. Walker 1990; Timmins 1995). Here the theory of abusive families met with the reality of women's experience. In a context where safety was assured, women began to disclose their personal pain and suffering, on the job, at university, and within consciousness-raising groups, or in therapy. And their stories fueled the passion of activists, creating both an intense emotional fervor and a call for immediate social action.

This feminist wake-up call to the reality of battery led to the emergence of the transition house movement (G. Walker 1990). Predicated on the notion that women who lived with violent men need safety and respite, the transition house movement offers a victimized woman and her dependent children temporary refuge, as well as information and counseling. Conceptualized as a male problem of power, feminists do not regard abuse as a family issue, nor do they regard women and men as co-partners in its solution (Thorne-Finch 1992).

Though it is activist in orientation, the transition house movement and feminists who lobby on its behalf are committed to a reconceptualization of the private fear of an individual battered woman into a public issue of violence against women (Loeske 1992). And it is on this issue that there is marked resistance (Timmins 1995; Harrison and Laliberté 1994). Within the feminist framework, woman abuse is believed to be a specific example of male power and privilege, persistent and ongoing evidence of inequitable gender relations within marriage and within the broader culture (DeKeseredy and MacLeod 1998; Dobash and Dobash 1979). At the heart of the shelter movement's feminist underpinnings is a critique of modern culture and a skepticism of the *Brady Bunch*. Through its provision of temporary service, the transition house movement seeks to offer abused women a second chance — an opportunity to gain control over their lives and to start anew apart from the partners who threaten their physical and emotional health. But, as we shall see, the story is a bit more complicated.

In recent decades, transition houses have gained a certain degree of popular support, their number has increased exponentially, though so too have their waiting lists. In the enthusiasm of communities to provide some resources for women's temporary shelter, and a myriad of professionals to assist victimized women, the feminist analysis has been all but lost (Timmins 1995). In the words of Jan Barnsley (1995), the voices of the caregivers have drowned out the voices of the victims. Some claim that the feminist train has been hijacked, as politicians, professionals, and police have appropriated selected features of women's pain under their occupational power (Untinen 1995; Loeske 1992).

To be quite blunt, most feminists see clergy and churches as central ingredients in any explanation of the problems battered women face (Brown and Bohn 1989). They do not conceptualize them as part of the solution. They interpret religious enthusiasm for family values as ample evidence that the sacred sphere is not a safe place for women. In large measure, the feminist founders of the transition house movement wince at its current direction and the dilution of its poignant analysis of male gender power (Timmins 1995). From this perspective, the main streaming of shelters — its social action success — has led to its ideological malaise.

A little later we will return to this issue of boundaries, cultural fences that are erected and maintained to ensure that the sheep are separated from the goats. Yet, part of the modern experience is a vanishing of boundaries, as fiscal and other structural realities shape institutions and people, negotiating the terrain between the sacred and the secular (Nason-Clark 2000b). Thus, the reality of cultural bridges mitigates against ideological isolation and exclusivity for the cause of the shelter movement. The harsh reality of home-life has now been etched on the conscience of many North Americans; but does a holy hush still pervade the churches (Nason-Clark 1999a, 2000a)?

The Story from the Front Lines at Transition Houses

When women seek shelter at a transition house, they are full of fear: fear for their physical health and their emotional well-being; fear for their children; fear of retaliation; fear of the future; they are also fearful of what others will think, fear the economic insecurity in the days ahead, and fear the termination of a relationship that at one point brought them happiness (Martin 1981; *Fire in the rose project* 1994). Most women who work as counselors in a shelter have been abused at some point: thus, their knowledge of violence is shaped by their own experience and the numerous narratives they have heard from women residents. Unlike the professional women who serve as board members for a transition house, or the lobbyists who founded it, they are not normally university educated, nor do they espouse a particularly feminist interpretation of contemporary society. Rather, counselors at these houses conceptualize abuse primarily through the lives of women they know personally, or whose stories they have heard retold by others.

As a result, shelter workers know all too well of the confusion and conflicting loyalties surrounding an individual battered wife. She wants the violence to stop, but she may not want to terminate the relationship. She wants her mental health restored, but she may not want to move out of a context that threatens her emotional well-being. She wants her children to grow up in a non-abusive family context, but she does not want them to be father-less. She wants to journey towards healing. She wants the future to look brighter than the past. She wants to live without danger or fear. She often wants to go back home.

Shelter workers often feel isolated from mainstream care giving in the community. They work with very limited budgets, their funding base is rarely assured, their care is at best temporary, and the needs of the children of abused women are often overlooked. Their services are rarely well integrated with the justice system, policing, or the emergency department of the local hospital. In a sense, these counsellors work as a stop-gap measure: attempting with very good intentions to temporarily bandage what years of neglect and abuse have caused.

Violated women in a shelter environment come with a myriad of social service and mental health needs. We must remember that women who seek shelter at a transition house do so because they have no other alternative. If they had access to a gold card, or a separate banking account, they would stay at a hotel; if their network of support included family and friends with ample space in their homes, they would seek refuge there. For the most part, and there are notable exceptions, of course, women who flee to a shelter do so as a last resort. They are economically or socially vulnerable women, though their partners may or may not be without resources. Frequently, they are separated from family and support networks, by either geography or the social isolation imposed upon them by their abuser or the shame he has created. If we are to understand fully the complex web of abuse, we need to realize that while violence knows no social class, ethnic, age, or faith boundaries, it impacts women differently.

The experience of abuse, one shared by about one in three women in Canada (Statistics Canada 1993) and the United States (Straus and Gelles 1986), has some overlapping features experienced by most women victims: the fear; the shame; the vulnerability; the long-term consequences of the pain; and the arduous healing journey. While Mary Shawn Copeland argues that all women live with the fear or reality of violence (Copeland 1994), an individual woman's personal narrative and characteristics, including the importance of her religious faith, shape her disclosure of that abuse and the road she travels in her quest for wholeness (cf., Fiorenza 1994; Halsey 1984; Clarke 1986). Women who inhabit very closed religious or ethnic communities are especially vulnerable *when* abused, though the incidence rates of that abuse may approximate those of other women (Nason-Clark 1995; Miedema and Wachholz 1998). They are more likely to disclose the violence within the community, and to be silenced if that disclosure does not receive practical and emotional support. Consequently, there are some unique challenges facing both religious and secular care-givers who provide assistance to abused religious women (Horton and Williamson 1988; Whipple 1987).

Does the average shelter worker have any contact with local clergy or churches? Through telephone interviews with counselors at transition houses, we learned that the most notable contact between churches and the shelter is mediated through the informal network of women's groups that operate at the parish level. At first blush, one would not expect these two groups of women to share much in the way of political, ideological, or religious worldviews. Yet, in a very interesting and inspiring way, they were able to set aside some of their ideological differences in order to cooperate and collaborate in helping abused women on their road to wholeness (Beaman-Hall and Nason-Clark 1997b). Understanding their work as a *ministry*, church women understood these ongoing acts under the umbrella of Christian social action. Whether it was comfort kits prepared for women residents, or the gifts accumulated by a "shower for the shelter," church women reached out to their sisters in tangible ways, not unnoticed by transition house staff. Clergy, on the other hand, rarely had contact with shelter workers, seldom did they bring an abused woman to the house, seldom did they invite the staff to make a presentation in their church, and seldom did they volunteer either themselves or church resources. While church women were busy building bridges from the steeple to the shelter, clergy were often found to be protecting the boundaries that isolated the church from the secular caring community.

The Story from the Christian Family Literature

The sacredness of family life and the emotional appeal of *family values* dominate the conservative religious market place, with Dr. James Dobson and his Focus on the Family organization its primary mouthpiece. With a staff of more than one thousand, Focus on the Family is able to publish and disseminate a wide variety of popular Christian magazines and audio-tapes, weekly columns that appear in secular newsprint and an average of fifty books a year (Gay, Ellison, and Power 1986; Nason-Clark 1997). Together with other popular Christian family writers, like Gary Smalley (1988, 1996) and the LaHayes (1978, 1982, 1985), Dobson (1995, 1996) teaches that God's design for family life is characterized by strong male leadership and submissive female nurturance, a message that has received even more press and popularity through the Promise Keepers Movement (Lockhart 1996; Elmore 1992; Janssen 1994). This blueprint for family living promises marital happiness, family unity, and extra strength to fight the external social forces that are supposedly seeking to *destroy* America's families, like divorce, gay rights, women's rights, and rebellious children.

It is important to declare that James Dobson never condones the physical battery of women by their husbands, but, on the other hand, he never really condemns explicitly the use of force. On the contrary, when there is the presence of excessive power and control exercised by men, Dobson holds the wife responsible for stopping the abuse through his famous concept, *tough love*. He advises battered women to stand firm, surround themselves with the support of family and friends, and to seek counseling from a trained religious leader. Within this framework, reconciliation is *the* number one goal of clerical or clinical intervention in the life of an abused woman and her violent male partner.

The other writers too, like Smalley and the LaHayes, who write best sellers for a primarily female audience, suggest that women look inside themselves when they have been violated. In so doing, they will find what Smalley (1996: 48) calls the *hidden pearls* in the offense that has been committed against them. Submission to one's husband, the LaHayes teach, is not "contingent on the actions of your partner" (1995:103). The message of *happy family living* is proclaimed loudly as the reality of violence is all but dismissed.

As of late, several researchers have become intrigued with the concept of wifely submission, Lori Beaman (1999) in *Shared beliefs, different lives*, R. Marie Griffith (1997) in *God's daughters*, and Brenda Brasher (1998), to name but a few. One of the overlapping features of their work is how women appropriate selected features of contemporary culture and the women's movement with selected features of the concept of submission. Most of the social scientists who study the concept of submission argue that from the perspective of the women involved, but not necessarily the men who advocate the concept, there is a persistent perception of a marked degree of freedom in submission. In fact, over the last fifteen years, Mary Jo Neitz (1987), Nancy Ammerman (1987), Debra

Kaufman (1991), and Lynn Davidman (1991) have argued that conservative religious groups may define women's roles narrowly from the feminist perspective, but they also define a role for men in the family, something that is perceived to be very important to female members. As a result, there is perception of equity in relationship and roles that women attribute to themselves and their partners. In fact, amongst my graduate students, Michelle Spencer-Arsenault, Lisa Hanson, and Lenora Sleep, who have completed fieldwork amongst Catholic, Baptist, and Pentecostal women respectively, there are some interesting overlaps in the appropriation of secular and religious models that women follow. Religious women perceive it to be fair when the men in their lives make an emotional commitment to the family and offer some tangible evidence to support their verbal claim.

Notwithstanding how women themselves translate the message into their own lives, the rhetoric of happy Christian families is firmly etched on the hearts of pastors, whether they be from a conservative faith tradition or not. In fact, somewhat to our surprise, we found that James Dobson's books often graced the shelves of mainstream clerical offices and that his name had wide-spread recognition, and support, even in rather liberal clerical circles. In one instance, I was involved in a consultation for a liberal denomination where the ministry leaders, many of them seminary professors, deplored the strength of the Dobson message in their midst. Let there be no doubt about it: the Dobson message is popular and powerful. And as we shall see, clergy often find themselves caught between the crossfire of an ideology of family life they are meant to uphold and the reality of parishioners in marital crisis (Nason-Clark 1996).

The Story from a Day in the Life of a Pastor

We have become acquainted with how violence impacts upon the average pastor, by working together with a variety of Protestant faith traditions (Anglican, Baptist, Salvation Army, United, and Wesleyan) where individual projects have employed a plethora of research methodologies, including mailed questionnaires, in-depth interviews, focus groups, telephone surveys, and community consultations. The survey data enabled us to learn how often, and under what circumstances, ministers are called upon to respond to abuse that is perpetrated by family members. Through in-depth interviews with clergy, we are able to document the advice and referral practices offered to parishioners. We heard of the struggle of the pastoral counselor, poorly equipped for the task at hand, and yet pushed to provide more pastoral care. As fiscal resources come under greater scrutiny in the public square, and waiting lists at mental health clinics grow, the free advice of the ever-available pastor is hard to resist. And yet, we heard church women complain that their leaders were unwilling — or at least reluctant — to condemn abuse from the pulpit and we heard church youth comment that dating violence is never acknowledged in their curricula. So, does a holy hush still prevail amongst clergy, or is the silence being shattered (Nason-Clark 2000a)?

The evidence for a *holy hush* amongst clerical leaders is four-fold: resistance to the phrase wife abuse; refusal to see church families as equally violent; reluctance to preach against violence in the family; and interpreting reconciliation as recovery (Nason-Clark 1999a:44-49). Resistance to the phrase *wife abuse* amongst clergy is no doubt related to the fact that the terminology grew out of the women's movement, the feminist struggle to name women's daily life experiences in the context of a culture that values men more than it values women. As Lori Beaman and I have argued elsewhere, clergy prefer the phrase *family violence* (Beaman-Hall and Nason-Clark 1997a). Ministers are reluctant to lay blame solely on the part of the violent spouse, preferring instead to locate the problems and the resolution firmly within the family unit, to be resolved by the violated and the violent working in partnership with one another. By their own account, clergy are untrained to deal with violence, and reluctant to refer parishioners to outside sources for help. They conceptualize the problem primarily in spiritual terms, and as spiritual leaders, hold themselves accountable to find resolution for the conflict and marital malaise of their parishioners. Only amongst those pastors with the most experience dealing with woman abuse, did we find referral networks and a team approach. Thus, where cooperation and collaboration was needed most — by inexperienced pastors — it was most unlikely to occur. Moreover, few clergy have ever preached a message condemning wife abuse, and most regard the faithful as less prone to violence than their secular neighbours and friends. Under fairly intense pressure from groups like the Promise Keepers to welcome men back into the churches, clergy are reticent to engage in any activity that would single men out for criticism or make them feel uncomfortable in the pew. As a result, their counselling option of choice is to attempt to help couples communicate better, understand each other's point of view more fully, and to engage in explicit acts of kindness more frequently. When violent men are unwilling to engage in counselling or alter their abusive ways as a result of clerical intervention, clergy report that they have failed as pastoral counsellors. Unlikely to account for the violence or marital unhappiness as a result of non-religious forces at work amongst the faithful, clergy believe that as the spiritual shepherd they ought to be able to bring reconciliation and recovery to hurting men and women. Since reconciliation lies at the heart of the Christian message, it is the counselling path of least resistance. Yet, clergy often find themselves caught between the ideal of family unity and reality of family conflict. While we found no evidence that clergy directly dismiss an abused woman's call for help, or underestimate the severity of her pain, by default, the issue is silenced, since it is rarely named and rarely explicitly condemned.

In other church corners, though, there is a rumbling that cannot be silenced. We have heard countless reports of clergy responding compassionately to the needs of violated parishioners. Many jeopardized their own physical or emotional health to intervene in situations that were volatile. Since many pastors are on constant call, and since the demands for counseling are increasing, clergy continue to be a major mental health resource in the community. While some see clergy as gatekeepers to other local services, others regard them more as spiritual specialists. Regardless, Andrew Weaver (1993) claims that domestic violence is the number one pastoral mental health problem facing the contemporary church. Poorly equipped for the task at hand, clergy attempt to use their interpersonal warmth and charisma (the reasons ministers claim people seek their help) to calm troubled waters. They go fishing with abusive men, they take hurt women to the emergency department of the local hospital. They talk, they listen, they visit, and sometimes amongst the most experienced, they refer. Often, though, they become discouraged when they do not see change. After a violent episode, when a woman may call her pastor, the abuser may be remorseful for the hurt and harm he has perpetrated. He may promise to change. His remorse is usually short-lived. For very conservative religious congregations, there are some distinct parallels between a believer's conversion narrative and the rather inauthentic pleas for forgiveness on the part of a violent man who is temporarily sorry for his anger and his battery. In religious terms, the woman and her pastor *know religiously* that God can change the heart of a person in a moment. Experientially, though, the woman knows about the cycle of abuse and the brief honeymoon period that often follows a violent outburst (L. Walker 1988). Unless clergy are relatively experienced at counseling abused women, they may be easily deceived by an abuser's manipulative ways, including the religious words he speaks to ensure that his victim does not leave the family home (Nason-Clark 1997).

When pastors say that God is not pleased with violence, offer helpful advice, or use their spiritual authority to condemn the battery, the healing journey of a victimized religious woman is augmented, when they fail to ask if she is fearful, or fail to see her financial vulnerability or her sense of hopelessness, the woman's healing journey is thwarted (cf., Jacobs 1989 for child sexual abuse).

The Story from Women in Congregational Life

Women have a rather long tradition in churches of working together, using a needle and thread, or flour and yeast, to help ease the suffering of their sisters, inside and outside the fold. Drawing its strength from Bible stories like Dorcas sewing for the widows in first century Palestine, religious women have often used their domestic skills to help others and interpreted their kindnesses as a ministry opportunity. Our data reveals that this informal network of sisterly support is one of the most dramatic ways that churches are responding to abuse in their own midst and within the communities that they serve. In essence, women see the suffering of other women and want to do something about it. They are quick to provide comfort and slow to criticize. They appropriate both selected features of feminism and church teaching in their conceptualization of abuse. Since most church women have been the recipient of another woman's care at some point in their lives, they know how powerful and empowering such gestures of kindness can be.

Let me illustrate this first by reference to a recent example from my own life. About a month ago, I was asked to speak at a church women's retreat, to a group of women mostly in their senior years. I delivered my address to about 50 women as they ate breakfast and smiled appropriately at my remarks. In preparing for this talk, I had asked my youngest daughter, Christina, who is eight, what she remembered most about her grandmother who had died just a year or so ago. She responded, "It's hard to go to our cottage with an empty freezer, isn't it mommy?" "Yes," I mused, thinking about how my mother had always baked cookies, cakes, and pies and traveled to our cottage before our arrival to place them in our freezer as a surprise. I mentioned this in passing to the women, as a form of encouragement for them as grandmothers that the legacy that we pass on is often the ordinary acts we do without much forethought. The next week, the woman who had invited me to speak, contacted me again. And you've probably guessed by now what she said. The women I spoke to wanted my daughter Chrissy to go to her cottage with a freezer full of goodies and so they had baked cookies, muffins, and bread to make sure that would happen. I collected them from her freezer, delivered them to mine, and we have been enjoying them ever since.

Throughout our focus group interviews, and in Lori Beaman's dissertation based on in-depth interviews that emerged from these gatherings, church women reported an impressive array of services they had provided informally to victimized women who were friends, neighbors, sisters, or members of the faith community. Church women were aware of the challenges of confidentiality in a closed community and the limitations of clergy-only counsel. Through their actions — accompanying a woman to court, caring for her children, providing lodging for the night when she was too fearful to return home — church women encourage more disclosures, for the home of another woman of faith was a safe place to talk about pain, despair, vulnerability, and hope (Nason-Clark 1998). Hope itself, is an interesting concept. And as Tracy Carr, a nursing professor, and I are finding, for ordinary men and women faced with difficult life circumstances or impending death, hope usually carries spiritual overtones, even though medical professionals are reluctant to link the two.

The Story from Abused Women

Abuse is ugly in any form, and wrong in any language. It involves betrayal, humiliation, and loss of self-worth. Women often blame themselves and cling endlessly to hope that the relationship will improve and the violence will stop.

Many abused women feel trapped, isolated, and guilt-ridden. Religious women tend to think that marriage vows are forever, that they promised God as well as their (now abusive) partner that they would work at loving their husband 'til death drew their work to a close, that the biblical admonition to forgive 70 times seven means a perpetual cycle of hope and humiliation, or that women's *cross to bear* may be abuse in the family.

These religious motifs, powerfully illustrated in the writing and videos produced by Dr. Rev. Marie Fortune and her Centre for the Prevention of Physical and Sexual Abuse, include concepts such as *forgiveness* and the *suffering servant* (see Fortune 1988, 1991). Other religious writers note the close connection between religious ideology, hierarchy, submission, and violence. Joy Bussert (1986) asserts that as long as theological traditions cling to submission as their model for marital bliss, then battering will continue to be the practice. Pagelow and Johnson (1988) claim that denial and silence in religious communities immobilize victims and encourage the actions of perpetrators, leading some feminist scholars to argue that the holy hush can be considered an act of complicity (Livezey 1997; Brown and Bohn 1989; *Fire in the rose project* 1994).

Battered religious women come with some challenging therapeutic needs that have both sacred and secular overtones. Having the violence condemned by their spiritual leader has a powerful impact on the life of a religious woman, an effect that cannot normally be replicated in a social work office or the local shelter. Too often, women are advised by secular workers, wary of clerical or religious advice, to abandon their faith journey in the search for healing and wholeness. Many agency counselors feel handicapped in their ability to work with religious victims whose values they perceive to be in conflict with certain treatment options. In fact, secular therapists report that they see little success in challenging erroneous religious ideation (Holden, Watts, and Brookshire 1991). Yet, clerical assistance alone has been judged by abused women as woefully inadequate (Bowker 1988; Pagelow and Johnson 1988; Nason-Clark 1995). As a result, religious and nonreligious service providers need to expand their referral networks to include each other (Beaman-Hall and Nason-Clark 1997a).

The lack of coordination and trust between churches and secular agencies poses several dilemmas for the abused *religious* woman. If she seeks help first from a secular agency, her religious needs are likely to be ignored or underestimated (Horton and Williamson 1988). Moreover, a community-based agency is unlikely to see her religious faith as a coping mechanism for her pain, and even if they do, secular workers are poorly equipped to employ religious language in a therapeutic manner (Whipple 1987). The advice, then, that she receives in this context often feels to the abused religious woman as incompatible with the advice from her faith community. Ultimately, the struggle to support women victims and to end violence requires both the language of the spirit and the language of contemporary culture. Feminists must take the spiritual journey into account, even as religious practitioners need to recognize that money, food, and shelter help to heal the pain of the past.

In conclusion, *the family is considered sacred ground:* that is the story from the burgeoning Christian literature produced for a lay audience, and mirrored in social scientific data which reports the close link between religion and family life (Ammerman and Roof 1995). *The family is not safe:* that is the story emerging from twenty-five years of feminist analysis. *The family is in crisis:* that is the tale from pastoral counselors, caught in the web of a rhetoric they are meant to uphold and the reality of men and women embroiled in marital unhappiness. *Women need shelter from their loyalty to the family:* this is the word from the front lines, as shelter workers strive to respond to the problems of abused women and their dependent children. *The family needs our help:* this is the call to social action perhaps never audibly proclaimed but enacted with astonishing regularity, as scores of church women reach out to hurting sisters, neighbors, and fellow believers. Finally, abused religious women, often reluctant to name what has happened, guilty for it, and embarked on the long road from victim to survivor, frequently say *"My faith has made me strong."*

As social researchers, our task is to listen, understand, analyze, document, and disseminate the multiple layers in the relationship between religion and contemporary culture. May we do it with scholarly rigor, personal passion, and a large dose of courage. For there is often great resistance to the message!

REFERENCES

Ammerman, N. 1987. *Bible believers: Fundamentalists in the modern world.* New Brunswick, NJ: Rutgers University Press.

———. 1997. Organized religion in a voluntaristic society. *Sociology of Religion* 58:203-215.

Ammerman, N., and W. C. Roof, eds. 1995. *Work, family, and religion in contemporary society.* New York: Routledge.

Barker, E. 1995. The scientific study of religion?: You must be joking! *Journal for the Scientific Study of Religion* 34:287-310.

Barnsley, J. 1995. Co-operation or co-optation? The partnership trend of the nineties. In *Listening to the thunder: Advocates talk about the battered women's movement,* edited by L. Timmins, 187-214. Vancouver, B.C.: Women's Research Centre.

Beaman, L. 1999. *Shared beliefs, different lives: Women's identities in evangelical context.* St. Louis, MO: Challice Press.

Beaman-Hall, L. 1996. Feminist practice, evangelical worldview: The response of conservative Christian women to wife abuse. Unpublished Ph.D. dissertation, University of New Brunswick, Fredericton, N.B., Canada.

Beaman-Hall, L., and N. Nason-Clark. 1997a. Partners or protagonists? The transition house movement and conservative churches. *Affilia: Journal of Women and Social Work* 12:176-196.

———. 1997b. Translating spiritual commitment into service: The response of evangelical women to wife abuse. *Canadian Women Studies* 17:58-61.

Becker, P. E., and N. L. Eiesland. 1997. *Contemporary American religion: An ethnographic reader.* Walnut Creek, CA: AltaMira Press.

Bowker, L. 1982. Battered women and the clergy: An evaluation. *Journal of Pastoral Care* 36:226-34.

Brasher, B. 1998. *Godly Women: Fundamentalism and female power*. New Brunswick, NJ: Rutgers University Press.

Bross, D.C., R. Krugman, M. Lenherr, D. Rosenberg and B. Schmitt 1988. *The new child protection team handbook*. New York: Garland.

Brown, J., and C. Bohn, eds. 1989. *Christianity, patriarchy, and abuse: A feminist critique*. Cleveland, OH: The Pilgrim Press.

Bussert, J. 1986. *Battered women: From a theology of suffering to an ethic of empowerment*. New York: Lutheran Church of America, Division for Mission in North America.

Charlton, J. 1997. Clergywomen of the pioneer generation: A longitudinal study. *Journal for the Scientific Study of Religion* 36:599-613.

Chaves, M. 1997. *Ordaining women: Culture and conflict in religious organizations*. Cambridge, MA: Harvard University Press.

Clarke, R. 1986. *Pastoral care of battered women*. Philadelphia, PA: The Westminster Press.

Copeland, M. S. 1994. Reflections. In *Violence against women*, edited by E. Schüssler Fiorenza and M. Copeland, 119-122. London: SCM Press.

Davidman, L. 1991. *Tradition in a rootless world: Women turn to Orthodox Judaism*. Berkeley and Los Angeles: University of California Press.

DeKeseredy, W., and L. MacLeod. 1998. *Woman abuse: A sociological story*. Toronto: Harcourt Brace.

Dobash, R.P., and R.E. Dobash 1979. *Violence against wives: A case against the patriarchy*. New York: Free Press.

Dobson, J. C. 1995. *Straight talk: What men need to know; What women should understand*. Dallas, TX: Word.

———. 1996. *Love must be tough: New hope for families in crisis*. Dallas, TX: Word.

Dudley, C. 1999. Significant research: When information has impact. *Review of Religious Research* 40:293-306.

Ebaugh, H. R., and J. Chafetz. 1999. Agents for cultural reproduction and structural change: The ironic role of women in immigrant institutions. *Social Forces* 78:585-612.

———. 2000. *Religion and the new immigrants: Continuities and adaptations in immigrant congregations*. Walnut Creek, CA: AltaMira Press.

Elmore, T. 1992. *Soul provider*. San Bernardino, CA: Here's Life Publishers, Inc.

Feld, S. L., and M.A. Straus. 1989. Escalation and resistance of wife assault in marriage. *Criminology* 27:141-161.

Fire in the rose project. 1994. What is abuse? Facts and stories. Ottawa: The Canadian Council on Justice and Corrections.

Fortune, M. 1991. *Violence in the family: A workshop curriculum for clergy and other helpers*. Cleveland, OH: The Pilgrim Press.

Gay, D. A., C. G. Ellison, and D. A. Powers. 1996. In search of denominational subcultures: Religious affiliation and "pro-family" issues revisited. *Review of Religious Research* 38:3-17.

Gelles, R.J. 1985. Family violence. *Annual Review of Sociology* 11:347-367.

Gelles, R.J., and M.A. Straus. 1979. Violence in the American Family. *Journal of Social Issues* 35:15-39.

Griffith, R. M. 1997. *God's daughters: Evangelical women and the power of submission*. Berkeley and Los Angeles: University of California Press.

Halsey, P. 1984. *Abuse in the family: Breaking the church's silence*. Office of Ministries with Women in Crisis, General Board of Global Ministries, United Methodist Church.

Harrison, D., and L. Laliberté. 1994. *No life like it: Military wives in Canada*. Toronto: James Lorimer and Company.

Hoge, D., B. Johnson, and D. Luidens. 1994. *Vanishing boundaries: The religion of mainline Protestant baby boomers*. Louisville, KY: Westminster/ John Knox Press.

Holden, J., J. Miner, R. E. Watts, and W. Brookshire. 1991. Beliefs of professional counselors and clergy about depressive religious ideation. *Counselling and Values* 35:93-103.

Horton, A., and J. Williamson, eds. 1988. *Abuse and religion: When praying isn't enough*. New York: D.C. Heath and Company.

Jacobs, J. Liebman. 1989. The effect of ritual healing on female victims of abuse: A study of empowerment and transformation. *Sociological Analysis* 50:265-279.

Janssen, A., ed. 1994. *Seven promises of a promise keeper*. Colorado Springs, CO: Focus on the Family Publishing.

Kaufman, D. 1991. *Rachel's daughters: Newly orthodox Jewish women*. New Brunswick, NJ: Rutgers University Press.

Kraybill, D. 1988. *The riddle of Amish culture*. Baltimore, MD: John Hopkins University Press.

LaHaye, T., and B. 1978. *Spirit controlled family*. Eastbourne: Kingsway Publications.

———. 1982. *The battle for the family*. Old Tappan, NJ: Fleming H. Revell Company.

———. 1995. *The spirit-filled family*. Eugene, OR: Harvest House Publishers.

Lehman, E. C. Jr., 1993. Gender and ministry style: Things not what they seem. *Sociology of Religion* 54:1-11.

Livezey, L. W. 1997. Challenging the theology of violence. Paper presented at the Annual Meetings of the Religious Research Association, San Diego, CA, 5-7 November.

Lockhart, W. H. 1996. Redefining the new Christian man: An investigation into books related to the Promise Keepers movement. Paper presented at the Annual Meetings of the Association for the Sociology of Religion, New York City, 16-18 August.

Loseke, D. R. 1992. *The battered woman and shelters: The social construction of wife abuse*. New York: State University of New York Press.

MacLeod, L. 1987. *Battered but not beaten. . . Preventing wife battering in Canada*. Ottawa: Canadian Advisory Council on the Status of Women.

Martin, D. 1981. *Battered wives*. San Francisco, CA: Volcano Press. First edition, 1976; San Francisco: New Glide Publications.

McGuire, M. 1990. Religion and the body: Rematerializing the body in the social sciences of religion. *Journal for the Scientific Study of Religion* 29:283-96.

Miedema, B., and S. Wachholz. 1998. *A complex web: Access to justice for abused immigrant women in New Brunswick*. Ottawa: Research Directorate, Status of Women Canada.

Nason-Clark, N. 1995. Conservative Protestants and violence against women: Exploring the rhetoric and the response. In *Sex, lies, and sanctity: Religion and deviance in modern America*, edited by M. J. Neitz and M. Goldman, 109-130. Greenwich, NY: JAI Press.

———. 1996. Religion and violence against women: Exploring the rhetoric and the response of evangelical churches in Canada. *Social Compass* 43:515-536.

———. 1997. *The battered wife: How Christians confront family violence*. Louisville, KY: Westminster/John Knox Press.

———. 1998. Canadian evangelical church women and responses to family violence. In *Religion in a changing global economy*, edited by M. Cousineau, 57-65. Greenwich, CT: Praeger.

———. 1999. Shattered silence or holy hush? Emerging definitions of violence against women in sacred and secular contexts. *Journal of Family Ministry* 13:39-56.

———. 2000a. Has the silence been shattered or does a holy hush still prevail? Defining violence against women within Christian churches. In *Bad pastors*, edited by A. Shupe, 69-89. Syracuse: State University of New York Press.

———. 2000b. The steeple or the shelter? Family violence and secularization in contemporary Canada. In *Rethinking church, state, and modernity: Canada between Europe and the USA*, edited by D. L. and M. Van Die, 240-262. Toronto: University of Toronto Press.

————. 2001a. Woman abuse and faith communities: Religion, violence and the provision of social welfare. In *Religion and social policy for the 21st century*, edited by P. D. Nesbitt. AltaMira Press, forthcoming.

————. 2001b. From the heart of my laptop. In *Beyond personal knowledge: Reshaping the ethnography of religion.* Edited by J. Spickard, S. Landres and M. McGuire. New York University Press, forthcoming.

Neitz, M. J. 1987. *Charisma and community.* New Brunswick, NJ: Transaction Books.

Nesbitt, P. 1997. *Feminization of the clergy in America.* New York and Oxford: Oxford University Press.

Pagelow, M.D., and P. Johnson. 1988. Abuse in the American family: The role of religion. In *When praying isn't enough: Abuse and religion*, edited by A. Horton and J. Williamson, 1-12. New York: D. C. Heath and Co.

Peña, M. 1995. *Theologies and liberation in Peru: The role of ideas in social movements.* Philadelphia, PA: Temple University Press.

Roof, W. C. 1998. Religious borderlands: Challenges for future study. *Journal for the Scientific Study of Religion* 37:1-14.

Smalley, G. 1988. *Hidden keys of a loving, lasting marriage.* Grand Rapids, MI: Zondervan Publishing House.

————. 1996. *Making love last forever.* Dallas, TX: Word.

Statistics Canada. 1993. The violence against women survey. *The Daily*, 18 November.

Straus, M.A., and R.J. Gelles. 1986. Societal change and change in family violence from 1975 to 1985 as revealed by two national surveys. *Journal of Marriage and the Family* 48:465-479.

Straus, M.A., R.J. Gelles, and S.K. Steinmetz. 1980. *Behind closed doors: Violence in the American family.* New York: Doubleday/Anchor.

Stevens-Arroyo, A. M. 1998. Syncretic sociology: Towards a cross-disciplinary study of religion. *Sociology of Religion* 59:217-236.

Thorne-Finch, R. 1992. *Ending the silence: The origins and treatment of male violence against women.* Toronto: The University of Toronto Press.

Timmins, L., ed. 1995. *Listening to the thunder: Advocates talk about the battered women's movement.* Vancouver, B.C.: Women's Research Centre.

Townsend Gilkes, C. 1996. Go and tell Mary and Martha: The African-American religious experience. *Social Compass* 43: 563-581.

Untinen, L. 1995. Safety for my sisters: A history of the shelter movement in northwestern Ontario. In *Listening to the thunder: Advocates talk about the battered women's movement*, edited by L. Timmins, 173-186. Vancouver, B.C.: Women's Research Centre.

Walker, G. A. 1990. *Family violence and the women's movement: The conceptual politics of struggle.* Toronto: University of Toronto Press.

Walker, L. 1988. Spouse abuse: A basic profile. In *Abuse and religion: When praying isn't enough*, edited by A. Horton and J. Williamson, 13-20. New York: D.C. Heath and Company.

Warner, R. S. 1993. Work in progress toward a new paradigm for the sociological study of religion in the United States. *American Journal of Sociology* 98:1044-93.

————. 1997. Religion, boundaries, and bridges. *Sociology of Religion* 58:217-238.

————. 1998. Approaching religious diversity: Barriers, byways, and beginnings. *Sociology of Religion* 59:193-215.

Warner, R. S., and J. Wittner, eds. 1998. *Gatherings in diaspora: Religious communities and the new immigration.* Philadelphia, PA: Temple University Press.

Weaver, A. 1993. Psychological trauma: What clergy need to know. *Pastoral Psychology* 41:385-408.

Whipple, V. 1987. Counselling battered women from fundamentalist churches. *Journal for Marital and Family Therapy* 13:251-258.

Winter, M. T., A. Lummis, and A. Stokes. 1994. *Defecting in place: Women claiming responsibility for their own spiritual lives*. New York: Crossroads.

Wuthnow, R. 1991. *Acts of compassion: Caring for others and helping ourselves*. Princeton, NJ: Princeton University Press.

3

Queering the Dragonfest: Changing Sexualities in a Post-Patriarchal Religion

Mary Jo Neitz*
University of Missouri

In *Invitation to sociology*, Peter Berger described the sociological consciousness as characterized by debunking, unrespectability, relativizing, and cosmopolitan qualities (1963:52). Berger influenced generations of sociologists with his view that the goal of sociology was to look beneath taken-for-granted assumptions, to debunk them, and lay bare the processes of social construction (1963:38). He portrayed sociology as a tool for this debunking, and told us how difficult the work can be. "How can I be sure, say, of sociological analysis of American middle-class mores in view of the fact that the categories I use for this analysis are conditioned by historically relative forms of thought . . . ?" Although Berger and Luckmann described this epistemological problem with a wonderful metaphor — they say that studying one's own culture is like "trying to push the bus in which one is riding" — at the same time, they argued for the separation of epistemology from "the empirical discipline of sociology" (1967:13). They wanted to build a sociology of knowledge that concerns itself with common sense knowledge, that is, what everyday people know as "reality" in their daily lives (1967:15).

One of the things that has happened to me in my career as a sociologist is that I have become ever more aware of how complex is the task which we have taken on. Even the idea that sociology is the tool for unmasking the taken-for-granteds of everyday life seems too simple. I am ever more aware of the extent to which our theories themselves are profoundly implicated in what Dorothy Smith calls the "relations of ruling." The theories themselves are not "clean," not objective tools for analyzing the "messiness" of daily life. The theories

* *I want express my deep appreciation to Nancy Nason-Clark, Lynn Davidman, Mimi Goldman, and Janet Jacobs for their encouragement of this project. Conversations with Patricia Monaghan have been invaluable. I thank Peter Hall for his collegiality, especially his willingness to read my drafts on short notice. I am grateful to Bobbi Gourley for her continual support of me and my endeavors.*

themselves and the understandings they produce must be called into question. The assumptions that undergird our own theories must also be debunked.[1]

It was my encounter with feminism that provoked a radical questioning of not only the way things were in the world, but also of sociology. Under the influence of feminist standpoint theory, I looked for "gendered analyses" that went beyond asking "where are the women," or "add women and stir" approaches.[2] Feminist analysts such as Dorothy Smith called for a sociology for women. Feminist theorists asked what would happen to the theories themselves, if we were to put women at the center of the analysis. Would that process suggest new categories and relations? Would there be a change in the ways that we understand the world?

Putting women at the center of our analysis did indeed provoke new understandings of many of the things sociologists study. Results of this process also suggested looking at different sorts of things. For example, the history department at my university hired as their civil war historian a woman who studies what the women did during the civil war — African-American women, and white women without property, as well as planter class women. As you might imagine, there were complaints from those who expected her courses to focus on military battles, but studying the experience of women during the war revealed how their lives were also profoundly altered by the changes that occurred during and after the war, changes that had enduring effects on southern life, even though the changes did not occur on the battlefield (Whites 1995). For feminist scholars of my generation, putting women at the center of analysis also produced — sometimes implicitly, sometimes explicitly — a vision of the world as gendered. A world experienced differently by men and women. And how were we to understand the world of sociology? Too often we experienced that defined by men for men. Who were we as sociologists? Dorothy Smith wrote about what she called "the line of fault" to describe the bifurcation of her experiences in the world of sociology, on the one hand, and her experiences in the world of women

---

[1] In their enormously important and influential work, Berger and Luckmann argued that sociologists of knowledge had attended overmuch to "ideas" and not enough to common sense knowledge. Their attempt to redefine the sociology of knowledge was predicated on the assumption that epistemological questions referred to theory and their desire to move the sociology of knowledge away from being primarily concerned with "intellectual history." However, at the end of the twentieth century, the question of "how do we know what we know" has in fact been defused, and the distinction which Berger and Luckmann made between ideas of intellectuals on the one hand, and common sense knowledge of everyday reality is no longer so clearly defined: popular culture has absorbed social science theories; social science now draws on popular cultural understandings and expressions. In neither case can we assume any longer a shared and taken-for-granted knowledge without regard for location. This shift is the basis for the movement from social constructionism to deconstructionism.

[2] A more formal name for the latter is "feminist empiricism." Advocates, for example, argue that including women in samples provides better tests of sociological theories. They believe that feminist sociologists can create a more objective science by including women. See Harding (1986) for discussion.

(1987). It was a description that resonated for many feminist women in the 1970s as we tried to build professional identities in what often felt like "the world of men," and at the same time to maintain relational worlds as friends, daughters, mothers, partners, and wives.

As feminist sociologists we sought to create a new angle of vision. We sought to "de-center" the very notion of objective science; we experienced the science of our discipline as masculinist science (Harding 1986). We saw it as socially and culturally dominant, but not as "objective truth." The project of decentering however, was not about putting a sociology of women in place of masculinist thought. Some of us came to understand that we were embarking on a different sort of project. We were not working on a "successor science" to take the place of what had gone before. And we came to understand we could not talk about "the standpoint of women" as if women were a single group. We listened to voices of the women of color talking about their understanding of knowledge as "partial." Patricia Hill Collins's influential book, *Black feminist thought* (1994) powerfully articulated a vision of a black feminist standpoint which reflected the thinking of those in the academy and the experiences and forms of expression — novels, journals, poems — of those outside of it. Voices from the postcolonial writers, splashed over from anthropology (Behar and Gordon 1995; Trinh 1989; Spivak 1988). We began to think in terms of the intersectionality of race, class, and gender. We began to think of our understandings as local, particular, and contextual (Geertz 1973, 1983). Some of us found ourselves moving from being "social constructionists" to being "deconstructionists."

One of the problems — or maybe it is an opportunity — of doing a long term project is that the world doesn't stand still while one conducts one's study. And one's frameworks for thinking can change as well. Poststructuralist thought challenges me; queer theory has become one of the tools I use to problematize the standard sociological understanding that "gender" is socially constructed, whereas sexuality is biologically given. Queer theory also pushes me to ask what it means to think of identity as performative, and what it means to define "queer" as transgressive of categories and boundaries (Butler 1990; Sedgewick 1990; Seidman 1996; Warner 1993).

In this chapter I want to present two moments in my study of contemporary witchcraft, one in 1987 and the second in 1996. These two moments provide a frame for examining some of the changes in the embodiment of gender and sexuality at the Dragonfest, illustrated by the appearance of women with horns, which I first observed in 1996. I also want to show how feminist theory and queer theory help in analyzing the cultural changes we can see here. Finally, I want to suggest some questions that arise out of the application of these theories to the sociology of religion.

FROM A GENDER FRAME TO A QUEER FRAME

I began my research on witches working out of a gender analysis frame. When I started this work on Wicca in the 1980s, I was interested in women and spiritual power. The question of the relation between women's social power and women's access to spiritual power came out of my research on Catholic charismatics (Neitz 1987). They subscribed to the normative position that women should submit to the authority of men, yet the women whom I interviewed claimed that they found the spiritual practices — including direct access to god — to be very liberating for them as women. But social theory suggested that traditions which allowed women access to spiritual power were always accompanied by restrictive social norms because of the need to keep subordinates under control and maintain order (Durkheim 1954; I. M. Lewis 1971). I started studying witches in a search for other "effervescent spiritual traditions," defined as those which take as of central importance beliefs and practices regarding the existence of spiritual powers and the use of them to get benefits in the here-and-now. I specifically sought out traditions in which women as well as men had access to those powers. In contemporary witchcraft, people practice magic defined as "bending and shaping reality." What I soon discovered rendered my original question moot: while the witches did not have restrictive social norms, they didn't have much order either.[3] However, for a sociologist of gender and religion, Wicca presented an interesting case, for a number of reasons.

In the first place, Wiccan theology/cosmology is goddess centered. That led me to ask whether women could have more power in traditions which imagined deity as female. I questioned how the goddess symbolism might constitute a cultural resource for religious women wanting to reimagine gender relations. Secondly, unlike some cultures with powerful goddesses in their pantheons, Wiccans espouse norms of gender equality. Equality between men and women is one dimension in which they seek "balance." Although equality and balance are always constructed through practices, everyone at least endorses balance between the men and women. Thirdly, it is a pro-sex culture, but, as I will discuss in some detail below, it is not "patriarchal," that is, heterosexuality is not tied to an ideology of male ownership of women and children or to a more diffuse idea of the legitimacy of male dominance in the sexual, or any other, realm. These factors make it a good place to try to examine the intertwining of sexuality and gender. Early second wave feminists pointed to patriarchal religion as a key institution for the social control of women, and one way that has been accomplished is through the controlling of women's sexuality (Young 1989;

---

[3] See Douglas (1973) for a discussion of the relations between restrictive social norms and social cohesion.

Rich 1980; Daly 1967, 1978). The example of Wicca helps us think about the possibilities of "nonpatriarchal religion" and "queer heterosexuality."

A Note about Words and Places

I use the words Wicca and witchcraft interchangeably. Both words describe a set of beliefs and practices embraced by networks of individuals, loosely organized, without a hierarchical structure. Witches' networks overlap with many others in a cultural milieu which includes women's spirituality, alternative healing, Native-American, and other new age movements (Neitz 1994). In many cases, the boundaries are shifting, the definitions changing. This is even more true today, than when I began my research. I studied Dianic, or feminist, witches and the Neogardnerian, or Neopagan, witches.[4] Both follow a yearly cycle, based on the movement of the sun, and see themselves as resurrecting the prechristian nature religions of western Europe. Not surprisingly, membership in both networks is primarily, but not exclusively, Euro-American. Neither tradition worships, or even believes in Satan, a figure whom they associate with Christianity. They argue that the prechristian (pagan) nature religions were also prepatriarchal and precapitalistic, and that the Wiccan revival offers models for more egalitarian and ecologically sound ways of living today.

Initially I sought to explore several dimensions of Wiccan groups. These dimensions attempted to capture key elements of cultural critique present in the work of some of the prominent Wiccan writers: a feminist critique, a political critique, and a economic critique. I was interested in finding witches who identified as feminists and who practiced in women-only groups, as well as mixed groups (with both men and women). I also sought out some groups which explicitly combined their religious practice with political activism. Finally, I looked for groups whose members had regular nine-to-five jobs and were relatively integrated into the dominant culture of consumer capitalism, and groups whose religious practice was part of a broader counter-cultural stance, often characterized by a rural, subsistence lifestyle, and a marginal relation to capitalism. The first dimension became a central factor in my analysis, reflecting what amounted

---

[4] The current witchcraft revival can be traced to Gerald Gardner, in England in the 1940s. Gardner said he was initiated into one of the few covens that had lasted through the centuries, and he claimed to be reviving the ancient religion of the British Isles. Gardner's origin account has fallen into disrepute, but most give him credit for putting together a set of stories and practices which were reasonably attractive and coherent enough to be transmitted. After the repeal of anti-witchcraft laws in England in 1951, Gardner published a series of books which made his ideas more widely available on both sides of the Atlantic. Kelly (1981) and Adler (1986:80-86) argue that most of "Neo-paganism" comes, directly or indirectly, out of Gardner. I use the term Neogardnerian to describe those witches who trace their practices to Gardner or one of his followers. "Neopagan" is a broader term, and encompasses those groups who use mythologies with fewer or no Celtic elements. For a description of the differences between Dianics and Neogardnerians and a discussion of the relations between them see Neitz (1990).

to two significantly different witchcraft cultures, with different associational networks.

In the summer of 1986 I attended a national women's music festival with the intention of making initial contacts for doing fieldwork among witches. Although I knew of witches in the university town where I lived, for both personal and ethical reasons I decided against doing fieldwork there.[5] At the music festival I met two women who had just founded the Reformed Congregation of the Goddess. I made arrangements to go to Wisconsin to learn more about their plans. My identification as a feminist researching questions about women and religion gave us an immediate common bond, although I came to learn that being a feminist was not the same as being a witch.

Also in the late 1980s I met witches in the Denver area. The Denver Area Wiccan Network (DAWN) included witches who lived along the front range of the Rocky Mountains in Colorado, ranging from Colorado Springs to Denver to Boulder to Fort Collins. At that time DAWN sponsored a neopagan festival, the Dragonfest, around the time of the August full moon. When I first attended the Dragonfest and began interviewing Denver area witches, most described themselves as adherents of Neogardnerian traditions.[6]

My difficulty with describing these two cultures indicates the intertwining of gender and sexuality. The Reformed Congregation of the Goddess defines itself as "explicitly feminist." I describe the Front Range pagans, however, as "not explicitly feminist" given that they believe in equality, but are reluctant to label themselves feminist. More to the point, while the two groups are distinctive in terms of being composed of only women, or of men and women, the groups could also be defined in terms of different sexual cultures. Although women who slept with men were tolerated, the culture at Reformed Congregation of the Goddess, especially in its early years, derived from the lesbian feminist culture of the 1980s. The culture of the Front Range pagans, in contrast, was explicitly heterosexual, stemming in part from their Neogardnerian interpretation that the practice of ritual magic necessitates sexual polarity. It is a heterosexuality, however, modeled on some prepatriarchal imagining, and looking at it may help us imagine a post-patriarchal heterosexuality.

---

[5] I had already had a student complaining to the dean that I was a man-hating, lesbian, feminist witch, on the basis of my having assigned Mary Daly's book *Gyn/Ecology* in a Women Studies class, and I wondered about possible repercussions from conservative state legislators. I also worried about possible ethical dilemmas arising from getting to know people in a fieldwork setting, and then being in a position of having to grade them in the classroom — fairly likely given the overlap between the Women Studies student body and the women's spirituality community.

[6] Denver Area Wiccan Network no longer exists as a organization, although the Dragonfest continues to be sponsored be a new organization which exists specifically for that purpose. In this paper I will refer to the on-going Wiccan community I have been studying as the Front Range pagans, although there is no specific organization by this name.

This chapter reflects a movement in my work on this project: It started out being about gender, about women and spiritual power, but I have come to believe that we cannot understand religion and gender without examining issues of sexuality. The comparison of gendered differences leads to a discussion of sexual norms and practices, and social control and alleged deviance. I believe that this movement in my work also reflects a dialectical relation between changes in the world and changes in our ways of understanding the world. At the end of the twentieth century, gender norms appear relaxed, and a wider range of practices is in evidence. In many contexts, however, there is a limit on allowed practices, and that limit occurs at the place where heterosexuality itself is called into question.[7] In most cases, however, that limit is never reached. The "heterosexual imaginary" prevails.[8] Despite changes in gender practices, we live in a culture in which institutionalized heterosexuality, or what Chrys Ingraham has called heteronormitivity, "the view that institutionalized heterosexuality constitutes the standard for legitimate and prescriptive social sexual arrangements," remains in place (1994:204). The story of the "queering of the Dragonfest" is the story of the disruption of those assumptions.

APPROACHING THE DRAGONFEST

To get to the Dragonfest I drive southwest out of Denver into Pike National Forest. When I first attended, the festival was held on Pikes Peak. I missed the earliest years, when it was held on private land. Through a witch who worked at a New Age Bookstore, I first learned about a Front Range Pagan Festival, thus named because it was organized by a coalition of witches who lived just east of the continental divide, from Colorado Springs to Fort Collins. This woman facilitated my registration, and in August of 1987, my sister and I found ourselves driving south to Colorado Springs, and then west. As we bumped along gravel roads, we attended carefully to the xeroxed map we had been sent along with a list of items for camping, rituals, the community "stone soup" supper, and confirmation of our registration. That year attendance at the four-day festival neared 200, and the organizers began to look for a bigger site. Now I drive through the towns of the foothills — Evergreen, Conifer, Pine — and turning

---

[7] For an interesting example of exactly this process in the area of sport see Downing (1999).

[8] Ingraham draws here on the work of Althusser (1984) for whom ideology represents the imaginary relationship of individuals to material conditions. Ingraham applies this to the structures of gender in a way that emphasizes the crucial importance of heterosexuality: "Althusser argues that the imaginary is that image or representation of reality which masks the historical and material conditions of life. The heterosexual imaginary is that way of thinking which conceals the operation of heterosexuality in structuring gender and closes off any critical analysis of heterosexuality as an organizing institution. The effect of this depiction of reality is that heterosexuality circulates as taken for granted, naturally occurring, and unquestioned, while gender is understood as socially constructed, and central to the organization of everyday life" (1994:203-204).

off onto the inevitable gravel roads, and into the mountains. The road follows the creek. My eyes light on the willows that border it, the meadows, the Ponderosa Pine forests, the face of the mountain. A born-and-bred westerner, this landscape is sacred and holds magic for me on any occasion.

In 1996, the drive was familiar. Although the festival had moved to yet another site, one which could accommodate 700 people, I felt that I knew this part of the National Forest. I turned into the spectacularly sited campground, almost automatically looking for familiar faces and structures, and checking also for what might be different. I stop my vehicle at the gate, and trade my paper registration for a button. I enter the campground observing the people with small backpacking tents like mine, beat up pickups with campers, and the not so temporary compounds, whole covens camping together with large car-camping tents, screened gazebos, flies erected over tables for cooking and eating, their areas festooned with all sorts of banners making political statements and claiming the space. In a central area is a space marked off for rituals, a large community area, with seating for several hundred people covered by rain flies, kiosks for posting work shifts and announcements, a notice board. Another fly covers the community kitchen, where juice and hot water and coffee are available. Tents are set up for the medical staff, "Grandma's Place" for the little kids, and for Kids' Fest with activities for the older kids. Further down the road, the endlessly fascinating tents of the merchants, selling handmade soaps, crystals, knives and swords and chain mail, drums, leather goods, ceramics, clothing, jewelry, singing bowls, massage. . . . Close to the center, and the line of toilets, is a camping area set aside for people with disabilities. Deeper into the camp I see more ritual sites, the "clothing optional" camping area, and a gathering place for late night drummers.

People of all ages throng the road. A goodly number in their forties and fifties, the men with long hair and beards, the women with long hair. A younger group in their twenties. Lots of children. Most people look "white" (Caucasian). Dress varies, but I can't easily visualize this group transported to the Mall on Saturday afternoon. With their bodies and dress they offer a visible resistance to fashions in the dominant culture. Some, although fewer than in the eighties, look like escapees from a renaissance fair. Among the over thirty crowd, hair is not cut with concern for current styles, nor do they appear to subscribe to dominant culture norms mandating thin and muscular bodies. Conventional makeup on women is uncommon. Among the younger adults, other body decorations such as piercings, tattoos, or face paintings are common. Men wear shorts or jeans and t-shirts, but with capes, and odd hats. Leather costumes, either of a Native-American or European medieval style are popular. Many men carry sheathed knives and/or swords at their waists. Some people walk the mountain road with heavy wooden staffs. Many women wear flowing clothes, with long skirts. Weather can be extreme at 8000 feet. (I usually pack my down vest, rain poncho, long underwear, plenty of sunscreen, and a sundress.) In the heat of midday, women wear tops that reveal lots of skin. Men appear in leather loincloths. When it is colder, men and women wrap themselves in woolen capes, long cloaks. People wear lots of jewelry: large chunks of amber, and semiprecious stones, headpieces with bead work and feathers, large ornate silver ornaments shaped into Celtic knots. People carry musical instruments. (I look like a visitor from the L.L.Bean catalog with my bandana, camping shorts, mosquito-proof canvas shirt, and hiking boots.) People are friendly, happy to be gathered in this place with people like themselves: what makes them marginal in the outside world is the norm here.

In 1996, one of the things that was new in this mix was a significant gay presence. Not that gays and lesbians had not been present before. But over the last decade, the gay and lesbian presence has emerged here slowly and in marked contrast to the striking lesbian influence among the Dianic witches I have been studying in Wisconsin.[9] There was an organized, although still somewhat marginal, gay male presence. Along with workshops on "herbs for women," "mask making," and "the history of the Tarot," an adults-only workshop sponsored by two gay leather men titled "The Sundance and the Scourge: The Ceremonial Uses of Pain" (described as being about doing magic through sadomasochistic sexual rituals) made it onto the official Dragonfest program. Other activities were announced publicly but occurred in the spaces for more spontaneous workshops and rituals organized at the festival itself. Another workshop organized by gay males appeared on the program under the title "HIV and Transformation: on working with people dying of AIDS." A late night ritual, a memorial for people who had died of AIDS, did not appear on the official program, but was announced at the kiosk. Also at the communications kiosk were posters for the rainbow network, and information about the rainbow pavilion with directions on how to find it in the camping area. It was not located in the more public market area, but rather in the clothing optional camping area. It was clearly marked not only with rainbow flags, which were common throughout the camp, but also with pink triangles. A number of the merchants offered merchandise featuring gay and lesbian symbols from interlocked male symbols, and interlocked female symbols, to pink triangles and labryses.[10] One woman had stained glass pieces inspired by feminist theologian Mary Daly's book, *OuterCourse*, featuring a large naked woman leaping over a

---

[9] Also in contrast with groups affiliated with Covenant of the Goddess. Beginning in the Bay area in the midseventies, COG is the largest and longest running pagan umbrella organization. In the 1980s it developed regional councils across the country, and has, from its founding, been inclusive of diverse sexualities.

[10] A labrys is a double headed ax, found in the iconography of early Mediterranean civilizations. Within the women's spirituality and lesbian feminist cultures it is a symbol of the power of the women leaders of prepatriarchal societies. For some, but not all, women, a labrys represents the power of the Amazons in particular. Although there is no historical basis for this association with amazons, the wearing of such jewelry — small gold labrys earrings, for example — is a subtle signal of one's identity.

moon. The few openly gay and lesbian couples appeared comfortable expressing affection with each other in ways comparable to those of heterosexual couples at the festival. There was little evidence that anyone objected. One exception was a grafittied exchange at the kiosk: someone wrote an objection to the presence of the Rainbow Network poster on the kiosk, eliciting a response of "we are here, get used to it."

As I will discuss shortly these things in themselves represent a change. In 1996, however, there was more than an emerging gay presence. There was gender-bending. There were men wearing skirts — not just men with bagpipes and kilts of earlier years, but bare chested young men wearing brightly colored, batiked sarongs. There were highly visible male-to-female transsexuals, in key organizational positions. Then there were, as I will discuss in greater detail, below, the women wearing horns. Dragonfest was "queer" in a way that it had not been before.

GENDER AND SEXUALITY AT THE DRAGONFEST

Yearly festivals draw together many segments of the pagan community: groups that come as covens, solitaries (individuals who practice on their own), the pagan party crowd, and the professional pagans who make their living within the craft doing body work, tarot readings, healing arts, and/or making and selling merchandise which reflects pagan sensibilities. People camp out in a remote location, which both makes it cheaper to attend, and reduces the risk of harassment from nonpagan society. Those who attend have the opportunity to participate in large group rituals, as well as workshops on topics that range from magical practices, to discussions of the history of various traditions, to discussions of issues facing the community. People who attend this festival from outside Colorado tell me that it has a reputation for being "serious about ritual."

The Dragonfest has a local and homegrown character. The people who come prefer it that way, and they want to keep it that way. In 1987, they invited a witch of some renown from the San Francisco Bay area to do a workshop and lead a ritual. The Dragonfest community was not happy with how that went, and they have not done it since. In this it differs from many other Pagan festivals. It is not like Starwood which brings in the Pagan elite, or like Pagan Spirit Gathering, perhaps the largest pagan gathering, or Heartland which, despite it smaller size, uses bringing in people with national reputations (in recent years musicians in particular) to draw participants. The Dragonfest started out small and local, held on some land one of the active couples owned, and it grew to its present size of around 700. Stars of the Neopagan world may come into the region for talks, workshops, and book signings, but they not are paid to do workshops or rituals at the festival, nor, for the most part, do they come on their own. Perhaps related to that, my perception is that things changed more slowly here than in other parts of the United States: the Neogardnerian roots of much of contemporary Neopaganism persisted longer here than it did in other places.[11] Local practices resisted Feminist/Dianic Wicca and Native-American influences longer. Sweat lodges, women-only circles, and body decorations — piercing, for example — showed up later than at festivals on the west coast.

Nineteen eighty-seven, the year I first attended, was the year the outsider had been invited. Despite that anomaly, however, the festival displayed the strong influence of Neopaganism of Gerald Gardner and his followers. The core leaders of the festival had trained in covens which used books of shadows written by Gerald Gardner and others in the Neogardnerian tradition. Several rituals I attended, for example, were taken out of the *Grimoire of Lady Sheba*.[12] Coven leaders addressed each other by their craft names, often with the title "Lord" or "Lady." (These titles are also used to refer to the god and the goddess.) Newcomers like myself were expected to attend an orientation workshop on circle etiquette, where various rules about dress (including what one could wear to a skyclad ritual — women need to wear a necklace symbolizing the eternal return), appropriate jewelry (according to rank and gender), and what to do and not do in a ritual circle were discussed. They also taught us a simple grapevine dance step to do in the ritual circle. (Over a year's participation at Dianic rituals had not exposed me to any of these rules!)

In the 1970s and 1980s women-only rituals, often sponsored by Dianic witches, were extremely controversial at Pagan festivals (Adler 1986). The first year I attended the Dragonfest there were no rituals for only women. A tradition has since evolved of doing rite of passage rituals, initiations into adulthood. There are separate rituals for males and females, but those began with a ritual for men.[13] While none of the witches I have met actually practice in the "ideal coven" (described in Lady Sheba 1972) composed of six couples, and a priestess and her high priest, when I first encountered them, most of the Front Range pagans adhered to the idea that ritual magic required a group of initiated men and women for "the balancing of energies."

While lesbians, feminists, and gay men in fact practice in single sex groups, the public stance of the Front Range pagans was that such practices simply were

---

[11] See for example Berger (1998); Bloch (1998); Griffin (1999).

[12] According to witch's lore, a "grimoire" or Book of Shadows was a witch's personal notebook, recording the magical practices as they were learned. It was supposed to be hand written, and destroyed upon the death of its owner. Lady Sheba was born in the United States, then initiated into a Neogardnerian coven in London in the 1960s. *The Grimoire of Lady Sheba* was the first "how to" book published in the United States, and it reflects the Neogardnerian tradition in which Lady Sheba was initiated, as well as a bit of Kentucky folklore. See Kelly (1981) for an interesting discussion of the publication history of Books of Shadows in the United States.

[13] These are different from the traditional initiations into the craft, which would occur within a coven. Some feminist witches believe that one is a witch by virtue of being born a woman and being aware. See my discussion of initiation practices in Neitz (1994).

not valid. The conceptualization of "balance" between male and female energies, a conceptualization based on a particular idea of what constitutes gender equality, cemented specific arrangements of sex/gender/sexuality, in which people who identified as male, had bodies that were recognized as male, and slept with women, were expected to engage in specific relations in rituals with other people who identified as female, had bodies that were recognized as female, and who slept with men. In the late 1980s, however, there was some tension between the implicit feminism, on the one hand, and the maintenance of heteronormitivity.

It is worth looking more closely at the implicit feminism and the practices of femininity and masculinity, as revealed in interviews with community leaders and teachers.[14]

Implicitly Feminist

The Front Range pagans I interviewed had little sympathy for the anger they saw in women of second wave feminism, and none of those I interviewed embraced the label of feminist.[15] Yet, they advocated a form of magical practice which emphasized the equal participation of men and women.

The following woman's response to a question from me about feminist witches was typical. "Those early women were very angry. Some of them are still very hostile, very angry. I think it is sad. They came in from the feminist movement and they were very, very angry with men."

Another commented: "I feel that this is one of the greatest flaws in feminist Wicca, is that they tend to project some of their own *personal* misgivings about the masculine side of the human race, and apply that to magic and I think this creates an imbalance. I can understand somebody's getting into not having anything to do with men. . . . But have a son, just have one son and you realize you cannot hate men. . . ."

Another woman also talked about balance.

[Balance between male and female aspects] has to be achieved internally first, but then once you achieve it internally, or at least are trying to achieve it internally, then you can work at manifesting that balance externally between yourself and other people, and even there — in groups of women, they must find their male/female balance within themselves and then express that male/female balance externally amongst themselves, even in just a group of women. And certainly to have that in a mixed sex group, the people involved as individuals must first find out who their animus or anima is, come to terms with that other half, embrace

---

[14] In 1987 and 1988 I conducted interviews with community leaders and public pagans — people who were known as teachers and or had healing arts practices or practiced divination in the Denver/Boulder area. I located these people through bookstores, advertisements in alternative publications, as well as pagan directories.

[15] This differs from what Berger (1998) reports from her observations of Pagans in the northeast over a similar time period.

that other half, and then the two of them, ah — within the one being — they have to proceed to make connections with the rest of a universe in a balanced way. It's a tough job.

These witches, while not feeling comfortable with what they saw as the "pro-woman" position of contemporary feminism, engage in practices designed to express the equality of men and women. For example, one woman described her holiday practices. I asked, "Does Santa Claus come to your house?" And she replied.

My kids believe he is a god of Christmas, you know, him and his wife. And I have things — I have an altar in my front room which I rearrange with the seasons, and at that point we have a Santa Claus and a Mrs. Santa Claus there, and we put all the bows and ribbons and things around them. They are surrounded by it to imitate the spirit of Jupiterianism, you know, which is really what Santa Claus is, a Jupiter type god.

Although these women do not explicitly identify as feminists, they do talk about a clear connection between their paganism and their support for women's equality. Several said that women relate to paganism because it affirms them as women. For some, being a pagan is consistent with practices which promote gender equality. As one woman said, "It is so important for me to stand up for women. I try to do it in my life, also where I work and when I vote."[16]

These woman also see Neopaganism as affirming to them as women, and supportive of their seeking out expressions of their femininity that are outside those provided by the mainstream culture.[17] This sense of having a feminine or masculine identity, but not conforming to conventional gender norms is evident in the following woman's talk about her understandings of masculinity and femininity and how it is embodied by pagan men and women.

Pagan women are essentially trying to be the goddess. They all look — well they are expressing their view of the goddess and likewise, pagan men should be expressing their view of the god, who's not this white haired, old [guy] who lives on top of a mountain, nor the [emasculated] version that the Christians are coping with; he is more multifaceted than that,

---

[16] Concerns about gender balance were also addressed in more public ways. In the late 1980s there was discussion among Pagans nationwide about the need to have a public presence as religious organizations in their local communities if they wanted to gain respect for their spiritual tradition. In various places, individual pagan clergy joined ministerial alliances, visited schools with informational programs, and volunteered as chaplains in prisons and hospitals. DAWN decided that they needed, as an organization, to raise money to contribute to a community based charity. The charity they chose was a local battered women's shelter, because they felt that in that location their money would help "restore balance" in nature by helping to restore the balance between men and women.

[17] Eller (1993) has suggested that women involved in the women's spirituality movement are looking for alternative understandings of femininity because they are unsuccessful at the conventional ones. My data does not let me assess how successful the women were at conventional femininity, but their presentation of self was of women who violated the conventional definitions while maintaining a sense of being women in a gendered universe.

just as the goddess is more multifaceted than the Virgin Mary, although she's the only goddess we've got left in mainstream religion. And so, once you find an internal balance, you don't have to play stupid games, you can BE. And for many women, not all, but many, that means taking that feminine expression and creating something that feels comfortable to them:

> . . . There are too many women in this lifetime who have an artificial view of what feminine is, as what the patriarchy has told them feminine is, and they are doing this Tammy Faye Bakker number. And, that doesn't work, and then they think the answer to that is like, 'if this isn't working, if this is an uncomfortable mode, then my answer is to wear business suits and carry a briefcase.' And that probably isn't real comfortable either, Reeboks aside (laughs). So, perhaps what the pagan woman is trying to do for women, and for men, is to help them find an expression of the masculine or the feminine, on the surface — externally — that they can present what they're comfortable with.

When I asked her explicitly about men in the Craft, she replied as follows.

> I know a fair number of men in the Craft, because I've always been involved in mixed sex Craft, and most of them, with very few exceptions, are not the standard, traditional, currently available, street model men. They are generally more open, more willing to change. Patriarchy is just as crippling for men as it is for women. It's just that most men don't understand that. They're in a gilded cage, so they think it's a nice cage. The men who are in the Craft are aware that it's a cage — (laughs). Gilded or not, it's still a cage. And they are trying to find a way out. They are much more willing, most of them, to be flexible and to change. . . . There are men now who are trying, for their own reasons — for their own healing, for their own sense of wholeness. I know men who feel that they have been robbed of having a feminine half, and being told culturally that any kind of female behavior was wrong for them, and they are reclaiming their right to have a feminine side. But they are also now freer to find an expression for their masculine energy that makes them feel comfortable and find an expression for their female energy that is more balanced and more true to themselves.

In these interviews pagan men and women see themselves resisting conventional gender norms, but there is still an essentialism in the way that they think about gender itself. And that essentialism is verbalized most clearly in defining sexual relations, as we can see in the following interview segment.

> You need to have a balance. It is not that one is better than the other. But we believe the feminine is a little bit more important than the masculine. That is because women give birth. And you have to have birth before you can have death. Birth comes first. You have to have birth and then the rest follows. So that gives her a very slight edge. We know that a long time ago people worshiped the goddess. This was before any one knew anything about the male role in procreation. All we knew was of the female role. And so when we worshiped a divinity it was female after the female part in creating new life. What the feminists have done is to go back to that tradition. That's okay. It is a perfectly legitimate tradition, but for me it is incomplete. We learned about the male role in procreation. And so the people who worshiped the goddess began to add a male figure to that. They included the horned god. At first the horned god was the consort of the goddess. . . . But women can relate to it [pagan tradition] because they can identify with the goddess. And men can relate to it to because they can identify with the horned god. They can relate to it as the lover of the goddess.

In her discussion there is the unquestioned assumption of heteronormitivity. The defining characteristic of what it is to be defined as men and women is their (hetero-) sexuality.

Sexuality in the Central Myth

For witches part of observing nature is observing the changes of seasons. One version of the Neogardnerian story recites this circle of birth, death, and rebirth. In the cycle of the year the goddess gives birth to her son the god, in the dark of winter, at the winter solstice. The god grows in power through Candlemas (2 February) to the spring. At the vernal equinox the god and goddess are in balance. Beltane (May eve) is a celebration of god and goddess mating, of fertility. At the summer solstice (21 June) god and goddess unite "in the love that is death." Lammas (1 August) is a harvest festival — first fruits, yet first fears of winter, the god is leaving. Mabon (Fall equinox) is harvest — acknowledgment of the god's presence in the underworld. Hallowmas, end of the year, is a visit to the king of darkness, but it is also the time of conception of the sun child (Starhawk 1979:169-184).

Divine union is critical to this story. In abstract terms, it is union with the life force, symbolized as union with the goddess. In the mythologies that have come down to us, many cultures express this as a sexual union. Sexual union between the god and the goddess can be reproduced in ritual by a priest and priestess with varying degrees of approximation. But the act of sex between any two people (not the god and the goddess) is also seen as a way of "raising power" or achieving the divine ecstasy that is basic to the religious practice.

While Wiccan discourse is full of references to "the Great Rite," actual sexual intercourse rarely — if ever — occurs in public rituals. Symbolic sex, on the other hand is frequently present. For example, in ritual, swords or knives or wands or candles are often symbolically plunged into chalices. The rituals sometimes feature the passing of a symbolic kiss around the circle, and may be conducted "skyclad" (in the nude). Furthermore, they are performed in the context of a belief system that affirms sexuality and uses sexual symbolism to achieve a state of ecstasy. Goddess is life and birth; the God is death, but death seen as necessary and leading to rebirth. In spring the god is a pan figure, young and playful, but sexual. In summer the god is often visualized as the stag, magnificent and powerful. Yet, he never possesses the goddess — it is he who dies in the fall, to be reborn of the eternal goddess.

Witches who are not so attached to the gardnerian version, offer formulations which are less rooted in hetero-gendered assumptions than this one. For example, Starhawk, a noted witch, also sees divine ecstasy at the heart of creation, and creation is an orgasmic process: "Ecstasy is at the heart of witchcraft — in ritual we turn the paradox inside out and become the goddess, sharing in the primal throbbing joy of union" (1979:25). But rather than returning to an imagined heterosexual prechristian rite she expands the scope of the metaphor: "Witchcraft is a shamanistic religion, and the spiritual value that is placed on ecstasy is a high one. It is the source of union, healing, creative inspiration, and communion with divine — whether it is found in the center of a coven circle, in bed with one's beloved, or in the midst of a forest, in awe and wonder at the beauty of the natural world" (1979:26). These stories and symbols provide a positive evaluation of both men's and women's sexual expressions. Although often heterosexual, they reflect Gardner's nostalgic envisioning of a prepatriarchal, precapitalist utopia. They form the basis for imagining post-patriarchal sexualities.

Women With Horns

The significance of women with horns derives from the significance of men with horns. The cover of the program for the festival in 1996 is embellished with an intricate black and white drawing illustrating that year's festival theme of "Mirth and Reverence." A huge dragon wearing ritual robes holds a chalice in one hand and a ritual sword in the other. His widespread wings form a circle and within the circle ten men and women dance and drum in what appears to be carnivalsque revelry. None of the women, but three of the five men in the drawing have horns on their head; the elaborate branched antlers of the stag,[18] curling horns of rams, and the pronged horns of the antelope. In addition, two of the other men in the drawing wear costumes which include caps adorned with cloth "horns." At the festival itself, some of the men wear small goat horns attached to their heads, giving them a rather satyr like appearance.

The horns are a symbol of these men's identification with the god, a god to whom they often refer as "the horned one." Within Neopaganism a common name for the god in chants and songs is the "Horned One."[19] In rituals he is invoked and honored with a stance in which participants stretch out their arms, make a fist, and extend index and little finger. This god is not primarily a ruler or a protector. Rather, he is the consort of the goddess. He gives the goddess pleasure, and his sperm brings fruition to her fertility.

A widely used pagan encyclopedia tells us that "Perhaps the most distinguishing feature of a divine being used to be a horned head. Masks and crowns of incarnate deities were often those of horned animals — bulls, goats, stags"

---

[18] As Rhys Williams pointed out to me, technically these are antlers. The iconography of contemporary neopaganism, following its custom of freely borrowing from many cultural sources, does not, to my knowledge, distinguish between antlers (which are shed yearly) and horns, which are not. They invoke the god as "the Horned One" and have images of stags. The association of horns of bulls, goats, and rams with divinity was common in ancient civilizations of the Mediterranean and Middle East. Images of the stag may be more common among the Celts of Northern Europe.

[19] For example, one chorus goes "Hoof and horn, hoof and horn, all that dies shall be reborn."

(Walker 1983:409). Many images of pagan gods, of shamans, or warriors convey "male vitality" by showing them wearing horns of animals on their heads. Pagan men wear their horns as a symbol of their virility.

In Western society, the horns of the pagans came to have other meanings. The "horned one" came to be identified with the Christians' devil. Of course, there is another meaning in Western cultures of men "wearing horns," that of being a cuckold. Under patriarchy that has a particular meaning: it indicates the deeply shameful, and, even ridiculous, state of a man who cannot control his women. But it can only have that meaning under a particular construction of sexuality, one in which men are expected, by themselves and other men, to control the sexuality of their women, their wives and daughters.[20]

The horns of the men are an assertion of sexuality, which at the Dragonfest has been normative heterosexuality. In reaching into the past, however, into an imagined prepatriarchal era, they have created a culture of sexuality which is suggestive of a possible move into postpatriarchy. I am not saying that these witches do not have committed relationships, or that they never establish monogamous unions. But a "consort" is not quite the same kind of role model as a patriarch. Pushing it further, the image especially of the goat horned gods — Pan, Dionysus — calls to mind a celebration of ecstatic sexuality, of the body as a route to rapture, as opposed to seeing the body as something that must be controlled or denied to achieve spiritual states.

For women at Dragonfest to wear horns, then, is to claim for themselves this virility, this sexuality, in an act of conscious gender-bending. Both in their wearing of the horns, and in an apparently spontaneous revision of some of the choruses to songs, changing lines about "men with horns" into lines about "women with horns" the women "queered" the Dragonfest. Previously at Dragonfest, women had rights to sexual expression. Yet, at the same time, a heterosexual imaginary prevailed: sexuality was understood as gendered male and female. The gender-bending act of women wearing horns crossed a barrier that defined and separated sexuality as male and female. In wearing horns, the women transgressed the male/female binary: women with horns are not the same as men with horns, nor are they the same as women without horns.

This outcome was not inherent in the original Gardnerian formulations. As I encountered it among the Front Range Pagans in 1987, Neogardnerian witchcraft was a highly gendered practice, reflecting particular notions about

---

[20] Barbara Walker offers the following etymology which makes connections between the pagan practices of wearing horns, nonexclusive sexual practices, and the bird. She says, Cuckold is "derived from 'cuckoo' the bird of May, anciently sacred to the promiscuous May-games that medieval Europe inherited from paganism. The man who became a cuckoo, or cuckold, was one who didn't care if his wife was faithful or not, for both of them attended the May time festivities when the ritual promiscuity was the rule — or the fertility charm — as late as the 16th century" (1983:196-197.) Her sources — 19th century folklorists — say that the pagan men who participated in the rites wore horned masks and headdresses in the god's honor, thus the wearing of horns was associated with the cuckold.

gender — the need to balance distinct male and female energies. But, at the same time, those ideas about gender were not used to sustain male privilege. Over time more individuals reinterpreted the ideas about balancing male and female energies to stress the need for internal balancing of the male and female energies people carry within themselves. Feminists who wanted to have all women circles and gay and lesbian witches who believed that male and female energies were manifest in their single sex circles challenged the Gardnerian and Neogardnerian practices. In the current cultural context, the explicitly post-patriarchal beliefs allowed practices to open up between 1987–1996.

Queering The Dragonfest

How did it change? Gays, lesbians, and feminists — those who identified with Neogardnerian forms of Wicca/and or the Front Range community — pushed for inclusion. But that inclusion did not come easily. The tensions in the community can be seen through discussion of a workshop I attended in 1990. The Dragonfest program listed the workshop as "Gay and Lesbian Outreach." On the morning of the workshop, at the community meeting (these occur at the end of the community breakfast sponsored by the festival each morning) the facilitator of the workshop got up to explain that, although the workshop had been sponsored by the Gay and Lesbian Task Force of DAWN, the title did not convey how they thought about the workshop.[21] The speaker explained that a better name would be "Letting go of your fears of the other."

Ten people were present when I got to the site of the workshop. The conversation was at an impasse. On one side were two women who identified as lesbian. They were saying "Why do you care what we do in our circle, and whether it is the same as what you do?" Another person disagreed, asking "but why do you have to call it by the same name?" One of the lesbian women spoke out. She said when she first met the pagan community she had been struck by all the love, symbolized for her in the witches' custom of saying "we enter the circle in perfect love and perfect trust." She had felt that witches were a gentle, joyous people and was drawn to that. It felt especially welcome because, in her life, she had many experiences of exclusion, of people telling her what she was not, what she could not do. She broke into tears, then she said with anger in her voice: "How dare you tell me that I am not a witch, or that I cannot do what you do in my own way?".

The facilitator of the group led an exercise, and then wanted to talk about individuals changing. She said that everyone had to learn to be more tolerant of each other. There was some talk about the need for opening the third chakra,

---

[21] She seemed to fear that the title might be interpreted as an attempt to recruit by gay and lesbian pagans.

the heart chakra, that would allow us to embrace differences. My field notes read, "I left not feeling like 'fears of the other' were much lower after the workshop, even among the few who had attended. Still to have it on the program was notable."

In 1992 there was a discernable gay and lesbian presence at the Dragonfest. I attribute the shift in part to the conjunction of two very different events. In 1992 in Colorado, Amendment Two, an initiative to prevent communities from enacting anti-discrimination rulings that would include discrimination against gays and lesbians, was coming up on the November ballot. Ironically, 1992 also marked the 350th anniversary of the Salem Witch Trials. While rituals at Dragonfest commemorated the Salem Witch Trials, the talk at the festival was about Amendment Two. Many people wore buttons against the initiative; these were distributed from a booth in the central community area. At the booth the witches networked with others who were campaigning against the initiative. At the community meetings people gave speeches supporting gays and lesbians.[22]

Witches at the Dragonfest expressed a sense of identification with the gays and lesbians who were marked by the ballot initiative. There was a sense of linked fates which was based on a shared marginality: Not on the basis of a shared sexual orientation, but on the basis of a sense of shared resistance to the dominant culture.

I started this research with questions about gender. One of the things I wanted to know was in what ways the goddess symbolism, and access to spiritual power, could serve as a cultural resource for the social empowerment of women. I asked this question with some hopefulness, but also with skepticism, having knowledge of cultures where goddess symbolism coexisted with extremely repressive conditions for women. In this talk I argue what the witches are doing that is most radical, is not captured by talking only about gender, although it does have to do with gender. What is most radical is the challenge to heteronormitivity, a challenge initiated, but not fulfilled, by the evocation of imagined prepatriarchal heterosexuality, where sexual relations are not defined in terms of the ownership of women and children by powerful males. The conceptualization of prepatriarchal heterosexuality allows them to imagine what I am calling postpatriarchal heterosexuality. It is a sexuality which evades the hetero-homo binary.

---

[22] Several times I heard spontaneous recitations of the speech of the Nazi resister, Pastor Niemoller: "They came for the Communists, and I didn't speak up — because I wasn't a Communist. Then they came for the Jews and I didn't speak up — because I wasn't a Jew. Then they came for the trade unionists and I didn't speak up — because I wasn't a trade unionist. They came for the Catholics and I didn't speak up — because I wasn't a Catholic. Then they came for me — and by that time there was no one else to speak up."

LESSONS FROM THE DRAGONFEST

In our culture it has been easy to think that it is people of color who have race, it is women who carry gender, and it is gays and lesbians who have sexual orientations or sexual preferences. White, middle class, heterosexual men are "just people." They define themselves as the norm. Their race, gender, class, and sexuality usually goes without comment. Yet we live in a world in which the boundaries delimiting marked identities from those that are unmarked are increasingly ambiguous.

Queer theory is one of several poststructuralist theories that challenges the "binaries." Observations of the Dragonfest in 1996 provide an example that disrupts binary assumptions that there are two genders, male and female, and that people are either homosexual or straight, and that these terms have fixed meanings. The men in skirts and the women in horns suggest a fluidity of identifications, of practices. The use of the word sexualities in my title is significant.

> What exactly does it mean, sexualities? The plurality of the term may be unsettling to some who recognize three (or two or one) forms of sexual identity: gay, straight, bisexual. But there are those who identify as straight, but who regularly indulge in homoeroticism, and of course, there are those who claim the identity of gay/lesbian, but engage with heterosexual sex. In addition, some people identify themselves sexually but don't actually have sex, and there are those who claim celibacy as a sexual practice. . . (Takagi 1996:245).

I have argued here that over the last ten years the Dragonfest has gone from a Neogardnerian and heterosexual gathering to a surprisingly diverse gathering. I have called this a "queering" of the Dragonfest and have argued that it illustrates the potential for change opened up by an openly sexual but nonpatriarchal culture in the current climate, and in a particular and local social and political context.

This talk is not about the pagans getting it right. I am not advocating that everyone immediately don horns. Yet through such actions, these Neopagans are opening up new possibilities for conceptualizing and enacting sexualities.

The language of "queer theory" helps us talk about those possibilities. There is a sense in which the idea of heteronormativity is not new. Certainly Mary Daly's works (1967, 1978) offer trenchant critiques — indictments — of how institutional religion contributes to the social control of sexuality, and the oppression of women. Adrienne Rich's essay, "Compulsory Heterosexuality and Lesbian Existence," published in 1976, also argued that the control of women's sexuality under patriarchy is accomplished through normative heterosexuality. In her analysis, heterosexuality is not a biological given, but is rather imposed on women by patriarchy.

Yet to say this again, to say it now, as the queer theorists do, is not merely repeating what was said earlier. In the first place, we still live in a culture in which heterosexuality is taken-for-granted. Some things have changed: there are fewer rules defining gender appropriate practices. Whatever unconventional practices a woman may engage in, it is still true that having a "boyfriend" legitimates her "femininity." In the context of conscious social and political challenges to conventional gender norms, normative heterosexuality continues to define gender, although the heterosexual imaginary prevents us from recognizing it. This needs to be reasserted to challenge the notion that "post feminism" is the result of the end of patriarchy, rather than an expanding and deepening of the critique of intersecting structures of oppression. Second, the formulations of queer theorists move us beyond the binary notions of previous generations of critics. For queer theorists, the alternative to normative heterosexuality is not gay or lesbian sexuality, but rather a fluid and shifting performance of sexual practices, where the enactment of a particular sexual practice does not lock one into a particular sex/gender identity.

The story I tell, a local and particular story, allows us to see gender and sexuality from a perhaps distant vantage point — that of the Front Range pagans. Their understandings of their own beliefs and history changed when they saw themselves as "queer," when they saw themselves as marginal like the gays and lesbians. The witches themselves did not necessarily change their sexual orientations. The transformation was not within a binary gay/straight understanding. But they saw themselves as marginalized, and at risk, because of their transgression of the dominant cultural norms. They saw themselves — witches and non-heterosexuals — on the shifting margins of the dominant culture. In this is the queering of the Dragonfest. The transgressive performance of gender by the ambiguously sexed women with horns continues the challenge to binary understandings.

It is my hope that what we can see from this vantage point helps us to question what we thought we saw from other, perhaps nearer, vantage points. The challenge of queer theory to us as sociologists of religion is a challenge to our own assumptions about the naturalness of male/female and hetero/homo binaries, and how these assumptions remained unquestioned in our own analyses. It is a call to develop gender analysis in the sociology of religion that looks much more closely at the construction of sexuality, and the ramifications of the social construction of sexuality for gender structures and practices.

REFERENCES

Adler, M. 1986. *Drawing down the moon*. Rev. edition. Boston, MA: Beacon Press.
Althusser, L. 1984. *Essays on ideology*. London: New Left Books.
Behar, R., and D. Gordon. 1995. *Women writing culture*. Berkeley: University of California Press.
Berger, H. 1998. *A community of witches: Contemporary neopaganism and witchcraft in the United States*. Columbia: University of South Carolina Press.

Berger, P. 1963. *Invitation to sociology: A humanistic perspective*. Garden City, NY: Anchor Books, Doubleday and Company, Inc.

Berger, P., and T. Luckmann. 1966. *The social construction of reality*. Garden City, NY: Anchor Books, Doubleday and Company, Inc.

Bloch, J. 1998. Individualism and community in alternative spiritual "magic." *Journal for the Scientific Study of Religion* 37:286-302.

Butler, J. 1990. *Gender trouble*. New York: Routledge.

Clough, P. 1994. *Feminist thought*. Cambridge, MA: Blackwell Press.

Collins, P. H. 1990. *Black feminist thought: Knowledge, consciousness, and the politics of empowerment*. Boston, MA: Unwin Hyman.

Daly, M. 1967. *The church and the second sex*. New York: Harper and Row.

———. 1978. *Gyn/Ecology: The metaethics of radical feminism*. Boston, MA: Beacon Press.

———. 1992. *OuterCourse: The be-dazzling voyage*. San Francisco, CA: HarperCollins.

Douglas, M. 1973. *Natural symbols: Explorations in cosmology*. New York: Vintage Books.

Downing, J. 1999. Welcome to the ball Cinderella: Investigating gender, race, and class through a study of the lived experience of women athletes. Unpublished Ph.D. dissertation, Department of Sociology, University of Missouri, Columbia, MO.

Durkheim, E. 1954 [1915]. *The elementary forms of religious life*. Glencoe, IL: The Free Press.

Eller, C. 1993. *Living in the lap of the goddess: The feminist spirituality movement in America*. New York: Crossroads.

Foltz, T. 2000. Thriving, not simply surviving: Goddess spirituality and women's recovery from alcoholism. In *Daughters of the goddess: Studies in healing, identity, and empowerment*, edited by W. Griffin, 119-135. Thousand Oaks, CA: AltaMira Press.

Gardner, G. 1974. *Witchcraft today*. Secaucus, NJ: Citadel Press.

Geertz, C. 1973. *Interpretation of cultures*. New York: Basic Books.

———. 1983. *Local knowledge*. New York: Basic Books.

Griffin, W., ed. 1999. *Daughters of the goddess: Studies in healing, identity, and empowerment*. Thousand Oaks, CA: AltaMira Press.

Harding, S. 1986. *The science question in feminism*. Ithaca, NY: Cornell University Press.

Herman, D. 1997. *The anti-gay agenda: Orthodox vision and the Christian Right*. Chicago, IL: University of Chicago Press.

Ingraham, C. 1994. The heterosexual imaginary: Feminist sociology and theories of gender. *Sociological Theory* 12:203-219.

Kelly, A. 1981. Inventing witchcraft. Unpublished manuscript in the American Religion Collection, Davidson Library, University of California, Santa Barbara.

Lewis, I. M. 1971. *Ecstatic religion: An anthropological study of spirit possession*. Harmondsworth, England: Penguin Books.

Neitz, M. J. 1987. *Charisma and community*. New Brunswick, NJ: Transaction Press.

———. 1990. In goddess we trust. In *In gods we trust*, edited by T. Robbins and D. Anthony, 354-72. New Brunswick, NJ: Transaction Press.

———. 1994. Quasi religions and cultural movements: Contemporary witchcraft as a churchless religion. In *Religion and the social order* vol.4, edited by A. Greil and T. Robbins, 127-49. Greenwich, CT: JAI Press.

Rich, A. 1980. Compulsory heterosexuality and lesbian existence. *Signs* 5:631-60.

Sedgewick, E. 1990. *Epistemology of the closet*. Berkeley: University of California Press.

Seidman, S., ed. 1996. *Queertheory/sociology*. Cambridge, MA: Blackwell Publishers.

Sheba. 1974. *The Grimoire of Lady Sheba*. Minneapolis, MN: Llewellyn Publications.

Smith, D. 1987. *The everyday world as problematic*. Boston, MA: Northeastern University Press.

Starhawk. 1989. *The spiral dance: A rebirth of the ancient religion of the great goddess*. San Francisco, CA: Harper and Row.

Spivak, G. 1988. *In other worlds: Essays in cultural politics*. New York: Methuen.

Takagi, K. 1996. Maiden voyage: Excursion into sexuality and identity politics in Asian America. In *Queer theory/sociology*, edited by S. Seidman, 243-258. Cambridge, MA: Blackwell Publishers.

Trinh, T. 1989. *Woman, native, other: Writing postcoloniality and feminism*. Bloomington: Indiana University Press.

Walker, B. 1983. *Encyclopedia of women's myths and secrets*. New York: Harper.

Warner, M., ed. 1993. *Fear of a queer planet*. Minneapolis: University of Minnesota Press.

Whites, L. 1995. *The civil war as a crisis in gender*. Athens: The University of Georgia Press.

Young, K. 1989. The imperishable virginity of Maria Goretti. *Gender and Society* 3:474-482.

4

Women and Clergywomen

Joy Charlton
Swarthmore College

I am at once an old-timer and a newcomer to the sociology of religion. My connection to it began in my college days, lasted part of the way through graduate school, and then after excursions to other sub-fields, I returned, some fifteen years later, to an early topic of research, a study of clergywomen. During this time the field changed most obviously in the visibility of women as the focus of research, and in the increasing numbers of women as the researchers themselves. Less obviously, but just as importantly, research by and about women and religion has illuminated our own lives, and the lives of women outside a religious context. In my own case, a commitment to seeing the world through a sociological lens, to using particular methods of learning about the world, to maintaining a persistent curiosity about the lives people lead, and in particular the way patterns of work and patterns of meaning are connected, have infused all areas of my life, including the work I do now as a teacher and, for a time, an administrator.

I learned about the sociology of religion first as an undergraduate, when I worked part of the time as the Book Review Editorial Assistant for the *Journal for the Scientific Study of Religion*. As I logged in the new books, typed the letters to reviewers, sent the reminders, and read reviews when they arrived, I came to know the sociology of religion in an unusual way and unusually well — and, probably, in some ways, more broadly than I have known it ever since. Meanwhile an acquaintance gave me a copy of Simone de Beauvoir's *The second sex*, and I took the very first course offered at my university on what we then called "sex roles." (I wrote a paper on the presence and status of women in the field of sociology: the answers then were that there weren't many women, relatively, and they weren't typically in positions of high status.) Discovering feminism changed my life. It named and illuminated circumstances I had either never seen or understood, it expanded the range of life choices I thought I had, and ultimately it directed my intellectual and scholarly agenda. All my choices of what to study, and often what to teach, have included women at the center.

A feminist sensibility also resonated with my choices of *how* to study. Sociology as a discipline seemed very quantitative. I learned my statistics as required, and sometimes very much enjoyed the satisfaction of closure that equations and final answers (numerically defined) bring. But for me the methods of study resulting in numbers created too great a distance between me and the world I was trying to understand. While I believe and teach that the nature of the research question should determine the nature of the methods employed, I prefer to choose research questions that allow me to watch and to listen. In fact, far beyond being techniques limited to research, I use what I know about ethnography to inform my current work as an academic dean, and I use what I know about interviewing to be a better teacher.

I chose a graduate program that would allow me a serious focus on qualitative methods, and then for my first solo project found a way to draw together my interests in both women and in religion. I interviewed a sample of women studying toward ordination in two seminaries, one affiliated with the United Methodist Church and the other Lutheran. This was at a point in the late 1970s when a number of Protestant denominations had changed their ordination rules and women began to go to seminaries in substantial numbers. It was a moment to capture the transition, to see how women would fare in new settings, how they would transform and be transformed by new arrangements. The ministry was familiar territory to me, as I had grown up a Protestant preacher's kid, and it seemed an especially evocative occupation to choose to study, compared to other occupations whose gender ratios were changing: only ordained ministry had been understood to be declared by God to be off-limits to women. I suspect this remains a reason why clergywomen continue to attract sustained attention.

And sustained attention they have received. There was very little social science literature on clergywomen when I first became interested. At the 1978 annual meetings of the Society for the Scientific Study of Religion and the Religious Research Association, for which the theme was "Religion and Sex Roles: Challenges and Change," there were no papers on clergywomen and three on the topic of women in seminary, one of which was my own. By the 1995 SSSR/RRA meetings, for which gender had come around again as a theme ("Women and Religion"), I counted over 30 papers presented on the topic of clergywomen alone, in addition to many papers on women and leadership and related topics. That is one measure of how the presence of women, and interest in women, has changed during the last two decades.

The faculty in my graduate program responded positively to my work on clergywomen, but the parts that interested them were not the parts that had to do with religion. They were interested in gender, and in a changing occupation, and even the analytical focus on contradictions and dilemmas of status, a symbolic interactionist approach following the work of Everett Hughes. But the study of religion was not their specialty and so it was not what caught their attention, and I learned lessons about the importance of mentors. They did not stand against my continued study of religion, but I wanted to work with my faculty advisors in ways that would keep us in conversation. Besides, I believed the conventional wisdom, which was that I needed to be marketable, I needed to have broader options, and a broader focus on work and organizations would provide that. I responded to the responses to my work. The importance of mentoring is often acknowledged, in the sense of positive guiding efforts, but sometimes the shaping dynamics of guidance are more subtle, but just as powerful.

In the research I subsequently pursued I studied work and organizations, always studied gender, and sometimes studied family. I (happily) studied or helped study, in various ways and on various projects, secretaries and bosses, lawyers and judges, college students and mathematicians, and nuclear security guards in the US Air Force. I have tried to understand work organized in corporate and non-profit business settings, court systems, educational institutions, and the military.

Still, fifteen years after that first study of women in seminary, I was curious about what had happened to those women I had first interviewed. I wondered if they had finished seminary, if they had indeed become ordained, if they had found churches, what kind of responses had they received as women doing their jobs. So I went back and found the original sample, all but two of them, and asked those questions. I asked them to tell me about their careers, and their lives. This brought me back to the sociology of religion.

The story of clergywomen of the pioneer generation is a story about gender, work, religion, and the church. Ordained clergywomen by their very presence as well as their actions in positions of power — and in this case in positions symbolizing and representing divinity — are involved in changing the nature of work within and for the church, and perhaps changing some fundamental religious understandings as well. From interviewing this group of women who went to seminary during the early stages of the contemporary surge, I have learned more about how understandings of gender are implicit both within and beneath awareness, about what it's like to occupy combinations of statuses, how difficult it can be to interpret one's own experience, how resistances to change are more often subtle than overt, about how the presence or absence of women, as well as occupational structures, frame career choices. I learned more about how women downplay gender as an identity when working in fields defined and organized by the men who come before them — and still think their experience is different from men's, though neither they nor the social scientists who study them can articulate or demonstrate exactly how.

Eventually, negotiating new territory can be exhausting. As I interviewed for the second time these women who went to seminary what struck me most forcefully was how many of them talked about leaving. One of the striking findings of this research is that of the original thirty women in the sample, 24 of them either never graduated, were never ordained, never took a parish position or had left the parish ministry at some point in their careers, either temporarily or permanently. At the time of the second interview, only twelve were in parish or denominational administrative positions. Those who left, temporarily or permanently, moved in a variety of directions: to be home with young children, to return to graduate school for advanced degrees toward a non-ministerial career, to take administrative positions in social service, or to take on special, non-parish but still official ministry positions such as chaplaincies or pastoral counseling. Some of those who left came back to parish ministry, or might yet, while others who have remained with parish ministry talked about leaving eventually. "Leaving stories" were a central feature of the second round interviews with this group.

My interest in the telling of careers coincides with a growing interest in the social sciences in "narrative." I have begun to think of life histories of clergywomen as stories within stories within stories, each at different levels of social organization. There are stories about a particular event, or conversation, or congregation. Those stories are told within the context of their telling career stories and life stories, which have their own themes. Those stories are told within the context of an interview, with the interview to some extent shaping the direction and content of the narration, creating another kind of story. Meanwhile the interchange occurs within larger collective narratives, such as the collective narrative of the successful career.

For a moment I want to focus on this collective narrative of the successful career. The clergywomen I interviewed recognize what we could call the dominant narrative regarding a successful ministerial career: the seminary graduate begins with small churches or an associate pastor position, subsequently moves to ever bigger churches, the bigger ones involving supervision of other ministerial staff. If truly successful, the minister becomes an administrative leader within the denomination. Note that a parish position — not a special ministry — is at the center. This ministerial career collective narrative follows a corporate and secular model of success. It is not "official" so far as I know, but it is recognized informally though sometimes tacitly by ministers and is recognized formally by scholars. In fact, the way we as scholars schematize clergy careers goes just this way, and it is exactly on this laddering that we have looked for evidence of differences in career patterns and of discrimination. Certainly our quantitative studies do this, and I do this myself when I plot out careers of my respondents and look for patterns.

The discussions of a "glass ceiling" for clergywomen, and the universal agreement by clergywomen (including the clergywomen in my sample) that such a ceiling exists, repeats and reconfirms the success narrative for clergy. There was universal agreement that a "glass ceiling" for women exists, still, within both denominations. Those in my sample believed that women are less likely to get the jobs at the biggest and most popular churches, and are less likely to get administrative appointments at the levels of district superintendents and bishops. The point here is that to recognize a "glass ceiling" is to recognize and at some level endorse the concept of the career ladder.

While the clergywomen I have listened to recognize and accept the narra-tive, they also resist it. They resisted it during their seminary days as they talked about their career expectations and their understandings of success. When asked directly about "success" their first answers describe the conventional narrative, but in the form of a denial. Ministry shouldn't be about numbers, they said, it should be about faith. When asked about their own definitions of "success," answers were usually abstract and ideological, having to do with a more personal sense of doing a good job. We might think about leaving the parish ministry, then, as a form of collective resistance, or as an inability to reconcile narratives. The conventional career narrative — the story of how one is to be a "successful" minister at work — competes with the narrative about the call, the spiritual content of the work, a narrative about who they are supposed to be rather than how they are to move up a ladder.

Moving toward special ministries such as chaplaincies or pastoral counseling, or toward work in the social services, may be a collective way of fashioning careers differently, of setting aside a hierarchical model of career building, of trying to find a better fit for their talents and their needs, of making choices that suit themselves rather than meet appearances of success, of "composing a life" rather than climbing a career ladder.

Meanwhile, collective narratives are not gender neutral. The stories we tell and carry around about appropriate behavior and character for women are not the same stories we carry around about appropriate behavior and character for men. These culturally-produced, gender-differentiated stories begin in child-hood, they stay with us, and they are elaborated. To think that women and men look to enact their identities in work situations in ways that are more consonant with culturally-produced stories about who they are supposed to be makes sense in the face of such evidence. The value of thinking about narrative in this arena is that we do not have to posit an essentialism of gender difference; gender as a stable but nonetheless cultural production is more easily visible.

Here is an important point. As scholars and researchers we collaborate in reproducing the collective narrative of conventional success. As scholars and researchers — myself included — we are most apt to think of careers — including clergy careers — in terms of steps and ladders, we plot out job moves in terms of church size and supervising position, we look for discrimination by looking to see how many women "make it" to the "top." To the extent that we do this, we ourselves contribute to the collective narration of what "success" is. Doing so doesn't make it easier for alternative models of making a career or living a life to find an acceptable place.

There is something about this that transcends the careers and lives of clergy-women. Women who have taken on careers in any field in the past decades have had to negotiate issues of gender, occupational structures, and choices about how to live a meaningful life. This is no less true of women who now study women and religion, who now find ourselves negotiating gender in terms of what we study as well as the organizations in which we attend to our professional lives. We work within conventional narratives — of theory, of method, of professional success — and, I think, work to create new spaces simultaneously, with varying degrees of frustration and accomplishment.

A final few words about making a difference. A feminist sensibility also resonates with the hope that social science research will not be just for ourselves but for others, that our efforts will serve more than our own career goals and intellectual interests. Some researchers are positioned in such a way that the results of their research can be put into organizational play in an immediate way and bring about immediately obvious change. I have modest expectations about what my research can accomplish directly. In general, what I hope is that what I do is added to what others do and that the pictures that develop by accumulation then contribute overall to positive changes in those areas we care about.

The place where I can more immediately see an effect of the work that I do is in my teaching, and even in my current work as an academic dean. So far in my own narrative I have left out the part about having a day job, as if all I have to do is think about my research. (At professional meetings, I've noticed, we often leave out this part.) In fact, early on in my career I took a job at a very fine and intense small liberal arts college. The configuration of the job has contextualized both the kind and amount of research I do. It has also meant that I have very smart students, students who later choose interesting work and become leaders in their fields. If I can reach them — if I can teach them how to use a sociological lens as they look at the world around them, if I can teach them to pay attention to detail and nuance in any social setting, if I can teach them to respect and truly listen to those around them — then I can make a difference.

I try to foreground those principles in my daily life, whether the activity is research or yet another committee meeting or a friendly conversation. I still love to listen to people talk directly about their lives, their work, the choices they've made, and I still enjoy the challenge of observing social spaces and trying to figure out what is going on. Data, in that sense, keeps me intellectually alive. It's even one of the reasons I agreed to take on an administrative role. I often describe my term as an academic dean as an ethnographic experience, a chance to observe and learn about my particular workplace in ways I never have as a faculty member. It is a job that gives me the opportunity to conduct interviews on a daily basis, or at least that's one way to think about it, and few activities are more interesting. And sometimes I even get to make a difference here, too.

5

Studying Close to Home:
The Intersection of Life and Work

Lynn Davidman
Brown University

My research in sociology spans several substantive fields — religion (in its institutional and extra-institutional manifestations), gender, and family — but it is united by my continuing theoretical interests in the creation of narratives of identity in circumstances of biographical disruption, and the epistemology of social scientific "knowledge." Methodologically, I have primarily relied upon ethnographic methods of participant observation, in-depth interviewing, and textual analysis in order to understand how the interplay of individual lives with social structures and ideological systems — especially those related to gender — shapes the narratives individuals construct about their lives in a variety of diverse situations. A continuing fascination with the ways that people experience the sacred in their everyday lives also animates much of my work.

My books, *Tradition in a rootless world* (1991), and *Motherloss* (2000) are based on narratives created by individuals whose experiences of biographical disruption shattered their culturally derived expectations of their life course. In the first instance the study highlighted the ways that people who adopt a religious way of life that is distinct from their parents' attempt to create consistent narratives that incorporate these changes into their ongoing sense of self. *Motherloss* focuses on the accounts of adults whose mothers died when these adults were early adolescents. Analyzing biographical disruptions such as motherloss and religious transformation reveals that people who live through these sorts of momentous changes are uniquely situated to engage in the narrative production of identity and the reinscription of meaning. The particular forms and substance of these stories reveal the ways that individuals' life stories are shaped by the larger social structures and cultural meanings of the society in which they live.

GENDER AND THE STUDY OF RELIGION

Tradition in a rootless world is an ethnographic representation and analysis of two groups of Jewish women who, in the context of two distinct Orthodox communities, move to Orthodox Judaism as a way of resolving dilemmas of female existence in contemporary society. The two communities, modern Orthodox and Hasidic, illustrate divergent strategies — along the continuum of accommodation and resistance — for constructing traditional religious communities in the face of the challenges of modernity. The focus on gender and on religion allows each topic to illuminate the other, revealing the gendered nature of religious beliefs, practices, and socialization, and the ways that religious institutions constitute themselves in order to attract gendered, secular individuals and offer them pertinent solutions to the predicaments of modern life.

A close case study of a particular community, even a small, minority group, allows us to see more general stresses and strains in the culture. Although few women in US society choose to search for fulfillment in Orthodox Jewish communities, the concerns of the *ba'alot teshuvah* (newly Orthodox Jewish women) are common nonetheless. Many women in our society similarly struggle to identify desirable models for nuclear families and to find partners who will help them create these families; puzzle about the place of work and family in a woman's life; and express more generalized needs for certainty and fulfillment. Similarly, although these Orthodox communities are marginal, they are confronted by those same features of modernity that challenge other contemporary religious communities, such as pluralism, differentiation, and the changing nature of gender and the family. Therefore, the religious communities' strategies for meeting these challenges and constructing new forms of religious worlds in secular society are instructive and actually provide relevant models for comparison with fundamentalist Christians and other contemporary "traditional" religious groups.

This study grew out of a deep personal curiosity: I had grown up Orthodox and had rebelliously left Orthodoxy, and my Orthodox family, at age nineteen. I originally undertook this research to find out why women would make a life choice that was so different from my own. I had experienced Orthodox Judaism as sexist; it had clearly limited my options of study and participation in ritual. I wondered why women who were my peers in many ways would willingly choose a traditional religious way of life in which they (literally and metaphorically) sat in the back of the synagogue. The project taught me to not assume that other women experience gender issues in the same way I do and to recognize that there are many women who seek a socially legitimated alternative to feminism, which Orthodoxy offers. By revisiting this site of earlier loss in my life, and recognizing that Orthodoxy provides other women with a profound sense of meaning and connection in their lives, I found new ways to come to terms with, and reintegrate, my own Orthodox background into my narrative of identity.

Researching and writing *Tradition in a rootless world* was the project through which I became an ethnographer and a sociologist. In the process of reflecting on what it is I knew about the communities I studied and how it is I *knew* these things, I moved from a naïve position of ethnographic positivism to a stance more informed by postmodernist concerns about representation and authorial authority. In writing up my "findings" I came to understand that any account I could produce would be a representation of my respondents' representations of their life stories. Social scientific reports are necessarily partial and dependent upon reducing into one dimension (textual) the data of researchers' observations and our interviewees' accounts. In order to present my research in the linear form required by the conventions of written scholarship, I could present only a limited, selective account that was necessarily shaped by my own participation in all aspects of the research process. These insights were shaped by my readings in two areas that converged in some ways on these points: postmodernist ethnographic theory and feminist theory. Feminist research, founded upon the collective realization that women have been marginalized as both producers and objects of knowledge, has developed the critical concept of standpoint theory, a perspective that meshes with the insights of postmodern thought.

THE GENDERED NATURE OF RESEARCH

My growing recognition of the importance of the author's social location in shaping the findings and products of scholarship sparked my exploration of the gendered nature of research in the sociology of religion. Focusing in particular on the study of new religious movements in the 1970s and 1980s, I wrote an essay, together with Janet Jacobs, asking what impact feminist scholarship (which was also flourishing during these decades) had on the development of research and theory in this field (1993). Highlighting three of the most central foci of research in this area — the origins of new religious movements, family and community, and conversion and commitment — our paper argued that studies that place women's experiences at the center reveal significant dimensions of contemporary religion that are unexplored in the mainstream research. Further, feminist scholarship suggests new meanings of conventional concepts such as power, religious authority, magic, and the sacred.

Feminist perspectives on Jewish Studies, co-edited with Shelly Tenenbaum, explores a similar set of questions about the impact of feminist scholarship on many of the disciplines that comprise Jewish Studies. As editors, we sought coherence in the volume by asking each of the ten authors to address the same set of questions about the state of knowledge about women and gender in her particular field (such as Bible, Jewish history, the Sociology of American Jews, philosophy, literature and so forth). We invited them to identify the scholarship in their field that uses gender as a central analytic category for the study of Jewish life; to consider whether and how this knowledge has affected the mainstream of the discipline; and to theorize about how research that uses gender in its analytic apparatus leads to a reconceptualization of basic concepts and paradigm shifts in Jewish Studies across disciplines. Most authors argued that the generally conservative nature of Jewish Studies has inhibited the empirical and theoretical incorporation of feminist scholarship within the several areas of Jewish Studies, making them lag behind the (albeit slow) progress of feminist scholarship in the mainstream disciplines. Nevertheless, in all fields, women have begun to produce new knowledge that, as it accumulates in depth and breadth, may ultimately reshape the content, theories, and methods of knowledge production in these disciplines.

By the time this volume came out, I had tenure at Brown and a home of my own. I was ready to tackle, from a sociological perspective, another major disruption in my biographical narrative — the premature death of my mother when she was 36 and I was 13. I was interested in uncovering this silenced experience in my own life and in engaging with others in the production of narratives of motherloss that would break their own silences about motherloss and our larger cultural silences about death. I wanted to know how others' accounts of their experiences were similar to, and different from, my own; I was in search of a framework and a language in which to script this unspeakable event. I began the intensive, challenging, and lengthy process of interviewing women and men about their experiences of premature motherloss.

MOTHERLOSS

Within U.S. culture, there is a deep belief, embedded in our social institutions and ideologies, that children are best reared through the intensive and exclusive devotion of their mothers. This book addresses the previously unexplored question of how this particular social construction of gender affects families in which the mother is absent. By listening to the stories of those whose mothers died prematurely, I was afforded a new angle from which to analyze motherhood and the family as institutions and as sets of practices. While the particular focus of *Motherloss* is the social context of mothering and its impact on people's accounts of their experiences of early maternal loss, the book's concerns are also situated within two other broad conversations in sociology. The first is American attitudes toward death and the impact of what Ernest Becker has called the denial of death on the formulation and articulation of these narratives of motherloss. The second is the discourse on narratives as a form of identity construction.

The book argues that a nurturing, caring, unconditionally loving mother is so central to our idea of family that people who prematurely lost their mothers felt that they no longer had a stable foundation for their lives. Their remaining families' deviations from the normative nuclear pattern resulted in feelings of discomfort and shame, which, in this instance, were exacerbated by the silences surrounding serious illness and death in our society. My respondents' accounts of motherloss revealed the lack of a culturally available language for speaking about death and for representing their "deviant" family forms, a lack that produced a sense of fractured identity. By engaging with me in the production of narratives of motherloss, respondents were able to revisit and reexperience the disruptive event, contextualize the experience, and integrate the narrative of it into a workable and mutable life story.

Writing this book was one way I sought to come to terms with motherloss in my own life. The research trajectory required me to engage in the same processes I was asking my respondents to do — to break my own and my family's silences about my mother's premature death. In order to do so I had to revisit this experience of profound loss, set it in the context of my own and my family's lives, and make sense of it in terms of the ongoing construction of my narrative of identity. Understanding the ways that larger social forces shaped this experience of maternal loss, and learning that my story revealed many of the same themes and issues that others' narratives revealed, was healing in some important ways. For me, this book was a way of thinking about motherhood in our society, but it also was a way to understand the meaning of this disruptive event in my life. I am a changed person for having completed this work; there is a basic sense of contentment in my personality that had not been there before. It is my hope that reading this book might prove helpful and comforting to others who have suffered such early and profound losses. My friend Susan Sered, an anthropologist, who also lost her mother in her early adolescence, wrote to me that reading a draft of my book was a "liberating" experience for her: for the first time in twenty-eight years she was able to talk about her mother without crying. Working on this book has made clearer to me the transformative potential of social science research — both for the individual researcher and for the participants in her study, as well as for the general society. The book concludes with a general analysis of the risks of both our cultural silences about death and the exclusive assignation of caretaking roles to mothers in nuclear families.

THE SACRED IN EVERYDAY LIFE

As a student of religion I had learned that Americans are typically more religious than their counterparts in other industrialized nations and that religion is particularly helpful to people in situations of chaos and terror, such as death. I was surprised then, to learn that the people I interviewed for *Motherloss* did not find their family's religious communities, beliefs, rituals, or clergy particularly helpful to them in their need to come to terms with their mothers's early deaths. Nevertheless, after serendipitously discovering that I — who considers myself "religiously unmusical" — had actually made what I eventually named a "shrine" for my mother in my living room, I began to see the numerous individual and spontaneous ways in which my respondents sought to maintain their mothers's symbolic presence in their lives. For example, one man sewed a piece of his mother's wedding dress into the *yarmulke* (skull cap) he wore to his wedding; a woman keeps her mother's favorite Christmas skirt hanging on her bedroom wall; another woman talks to her mother and seeks her advice during her daily runs. These attempts to maintain a connection with their mothers in their everyday lives were experienced by my respondents as "spiritual" or sacred, although the forms they chose did not necessarily derive from, or fit squarely within, the rituals and beliefs prescribed by traditional religious institutions.

Recently, students of religion have begun to recognize that religious practices and expression are not limited to the official forms provided by the major traditions and denominations that until recently have dominated the study of religion in the US. Recent volumes edited by Robert Orsi (1999) and David Hall (1997), for example, direct our attention away from institutional religion to the study of "lived" religion, an approach that highlights the various and complex ways that people act to create meaning within the practical, material situations in which they find themselves. By adapting a radically empiricist methodology, the study of lived religion focuses on those subtle ways that people, "in particular places and times, live in, with, through and against the religious idioms available to them in culture — *all* the idioms, including (often enough) those not explicitly 'their own'" (Hall 1997). The practice of religion is not fixed, frozen, and limited, but can be spontaneous, innovative, and assembled by cultural bricolage. Such an approach requires us to fundamentally rethink what religion is and what it means to be "religious."

In my next major project I seek to discover new, non-institutionally defined constructions, meanings, and practices of Jewishness among contemporary, unaffiliated American Jews. The deeply held bias towards institutional religious forms within the academic study of religion has dominated research on American Jewish life as well. In the wake of the Holocaust and the destruction of a third of world Jewry, the question of survival has become of monumental importance to American Jews. Sociologists of American Jewry seem obsessed with the question of whether modernization weakens the Jewish community, threatening its survival, or whether the changes brought about by modernization simply mean that new, vital forms of Jewish cohesion and expression have emerged. Within this modernization paradigm, unaffiliated Jews are seen as powerfully threatening to survival and as such become a residual category in studies of contemporary Jewish life. Community leaders, and the many research studies they fund, decry the large numbers of unaffiliated Jews and seek ways to bring them closer to existing Jewish institutions. I propose, instead, to closely investigate precisely these marginal Jews — who actually constitute about one half of all American Jewry — and to learn about the varied ways they might constitute "being Jewish" in their daily lives. This question, too, relates to my own life: having abandoned Orthodoxy as a teenager, and having grown into an adult who does not belong to a synagogue, I am in search of ways to define a

Jewish identity that is outside of the synagogue and other mainstream Jewish institutions.

Here I circle back again to the study of how individuals construct coherent narratives of their lives in circumstances of disruption, although here, the disruption is cultural as well as biographical. Non-affiliated Jews often struggle to construct ways of being Jewish outside the boundaries of those established Jewish institutions that attempt to impose rather uniform practices and beliefs upon the highly diverse American Jewish population. Rather than defining Jewishness in advance, and seeking to identify how Jews conform to the several dimensions of Jewish life that scholars have pre-defined, my study seeks to understand the multivalent and complex practices and beliefs of the so-called "secular" American Jews. I am especially interested in the ways that these individuals construct on-going, fluid, and multivalent narratives of Jewish identity rooted in the situations and relationships that constitute their daily lives. I expect that these accounts, like all narratives of identity, will reveal the ironic, contested, and ambivalent nature of religious meanings, as they are constituted in situations of relative cultural freedom for contemporary Jews.

REFERENCES

Abu-Lughod, L. 1993. *Writing women's worlds: Bedouin stories*. Berkeley: University of California Press.

Becker, G. 1997. *Disrupted lives: How people create meaning in a chaotic world*. Berkeley: University of California Press.

Behar, R. 1996. *The vulnerable observer: Anthropology that breaks your heart*. Boston, MA: Beacon Press.

Bellah, R. N., R. Madsen, W. M. Sullivan, A. Swidler, and S. M. Tipton. 1985. *Habits of the heart: Individualism and commitment in American life*. Berkeley: University of California Press.

Bury, M. 1982. Chronic illness as biographical disruption. *Sociology of Health and Illness* 4:167-182.

Chodorow, N. 1978. *The reproduction of mothering: Psychoanalysis and the reproduction of gender*. Berkeley: University of California Press.

Clifford, J., and G. E. Marcus, eds. 1986. *Writing culture: The poetics and politics of ethnography*. Berkeley: University of California Press.

Davidman, L. 1991. *Tradition in a rootless world: Women turn to Orthodox Judaism*. Berkeley: University of California Press.

———. 2000. *Motherloss*. Berkeley: University of California Press.

Davidman, L. and J. Jacobs. 1993. Feminist perspectives on new religious movements. *Religion and the social order* 3B:173-190.

De Vault, M. L. 1991. *Feeding the family: The social organization of gender as caring work*. Chicago, IL: University of Chicago Press.

Di Leonardo, M. 1987. The female world of cards and holidays: Women, families, and the work of kinship. *Signs: Journal of Women in Culture and Society* 12:440-453.

Edelman, H. 1994. *Motherless daughters: The legacy of loss*. Reading, MA: Addison-Wesley.

Ellis, C. 1995. *Final negotiations: A story of love, loss, and chronic illness*. Philadelphia, PA: Temple University Press.

Garey, A. I. 1999. *Weaving work and motherhood*. Philadelphia, PA: Temple University Press.

Geertz, C. 1990. *Works and lives: The anthropologist as author*. Stanford, CA: Stanford University Press.

Gilligan, C. 1982. *In a different voice: Psychological theory and women's development*. Cambridge, MA: Harvard University Press.

Gornick, V. 1996. Why memoir now? *Women's Review of Books* 13, 10-11 July, 5.

Hall, D., ed. 1997. *Lived religion in America: Toward a history of practice*. Princeton, NJ: Princeton University Press.

Hays, S. 1966. *The cultural contradictions of motherhood*. New Haven, CT: Yale University Press.

Kahn, R. P. 1995. *Bearing meaning: The language of birth*. Urbana: University of Illinois Press.

Luckmann, T. 1967. *The invisible religion: The problem of religion in modern society*. New York: MacMillan.

Marcus, G. E., and M. M. J. Fischer. 1986. *Anthropology as cultural critique*. Chicago, IL: University of Chicago Press.

Miller, N. K. 1996. *Bequest and betrayal: Memoirs of a parent's death*. New York: Oxford University Press.

Orsi, R., ed. 1999. *Gods of the city: Religion and the American urban landscape*. Bloomington: Indiana University Press.

Richardson, L. 1997. *Fields of play: Constructing an academic life*. New Brunswick, NJ: Rutgers University Press.

Rosenwald, G. C., and R. L. Ochberg, eds. 1992. *Storied lives: The cultural politics of self-understanding*. New Haven, CT: Yale University Press.

Sontag, S. 1978. *Illness as metaphor*. New York: Farrar, Straus, and Giroux.

6

Hidden Truths and Cultures of Secrecy: Reflections on Gender and Ethnicity in the Study of Religion

Janet Liebman Jacobs
University of Colorado

THE "FIRST WAVE" OF FEMINISM AND MY EMERGENCE AS A GENDER SCHOLAR

My research narrative begins in India in 1972. In the winter of that year I visited an ashram that had recently been established in a high rise apartment building in a wealthy section of Bombay known as Beach Candy. I had gone to the ashram expressly to meet the spiritual teacher, Bhagwan Shree Rajneesh, whose Sunnyasin movement had just begun to attract followers from the West. Among the small cadre of devotees who lived in his burgeoning spiritual community was a close cousin who had recently come to India to study with Bhagwan.[1] My cousin now called herself by a Hindu name, she wore only orange clothing, and her speech was punctuated with phrases of adoration for the Oxford educated guru. The day I visited the ashram, Bhagwan was giving a talk to a number of academics from the United States, and although I was merely a 70s traveler, making my way from West to East, he agreed to let me join the group of Western intellectuals. I remember clearly how excited my cousin was as she prepared the room for Bhagwan's entry. Her own small room in the ashram bore a plaster cast of his feet, but, as she explained, this religious icon paled in comparison with the actual feet of the spiritual master whose body contained the essence of spiritual enlightenment.

I had been at the ashram about an hour when Bhagwan, young, thin, and bearded, entered the room, taking his place on a chair that was designated for him alone. The guests were assembled on floor cushions and he smiled down at each of us as he greeted his waiting audience. After a moment of silence, Bhagwan began to speak quietly about his philosophy of life and the meaning of

---

[1] The relationship of cousin is used here to protect the anonymity of this family relation.

a spiritual avocation. I remember thinking that he had a very gentle manner and that his voice was soothing and calm. I also remember looking around the room during his lecture, searching out the face of my cousin, who was clearly enraptured, and wondering how she could have left her family, her friends, and her children to live with and serve this spiritual leader. I tried very hard that day, but I could not hear what she heard in his voice nor see what she saw in his starkly penetrating eyes. It was clear that I experienced Bhagwan as a man, while for my cousin, he had become a god.

The experience in Beach Candy was my first introduction to the world of joiners, followers, and converts. While I had no preconceived notions about cults or "dangerous" religious movements, the visit with Bhagwan and my cousin did engender a certain curiosity about charismatic power and the intensity of emotional bonding within small religious communities. Aware of Bhagwan's extraordinary effect on his followers, I left India with images of Beach Candy vividly recorded in memory, images of the Western style apartment building, of Europeans and Americans draped in loose fitting orange clothes, and of Bhagwan's orange Chevrolet convertible parked like a royal vehicle on the narrow streets of Bombay. Although these images and impressions stayed with me for a long time, they remained unexplored until I began my graduate studies in sociology nearly a decade later. By then I was living in a university community that had become a Western mecca for alternative religious groups. In Boulder I was surrounded by followers of Rinpoche, Guru Maharaj Ji, and the Reverend Moon, religious leaders who, like Bhagwan, appealed to a generation of young women and men in search of spiritual knowledge and community. At the same time, I was also aware of a growing number of individuals who were questioning their religious commitment and the choices they had made in the years following the turbulence of the 1960s. Fascinated by the changes that were taking place in the spiritual arena of middle class life, I turned my attention to the study of disillusionment and disaffection from charismatic communities.

As one of the first gendered analyses of new religious movements, my work, in all honesty, did not start out as a feminist interrogation into the abuses of religious conversion. When I began the study nearly twenty years ago, feminist scholarship was still in its infancy and the predominant religious emphasis was on critiques of mainstream denominations (Christ and Plaskow 1979). In good ethnographic fashion, I had begun my work by doing a qualitative research project on joining and leaving new religious movements. At the outset, I did not know that there would be such vast differences in the experiences of men and women. Early on in the project, however, I realized that gender played a significant role in the commitment process. The narratives of the female devotees spoke of attachment, rejection, sexual exploitation, and violence. By contrast, the accounts of the men spoke of jockeying for positions of power, access to women, and ideological differences with the religious leadership.

As I began to sort through these differences, I turned to the current research on new religious movements and found only one study that specifically addressed the issue of gender (Culpepper 1978). What was perhaps most problematic in the early literature was the tendency, particularly on the part of male researchers, to either ignore the data on the sexual objectification of women or to assume as normative, ideologies and practices that encouraged the sexualization of female followers. I can still recall the first time I read an analysis of the Children of God that described the practice of flirty fishing, a recruitment technique which encouraged and, in some cases, coerced women to use their sexuality to bring new members into the organization. In a 1978 journal article that documented this aspect of group membership, the researcher referred to sexual solicitation as an "innovative" recruitment strategy.

> How can this amazing innovation in religious recruitment be accounted for, and how is it justified by the Children of God? . . . Quite evidently, the Children of God have a considerably more permissive attitude to sexual matters than almost any other group claiming to be Christian. The letters of 'Father Moses David' have always adopted a rather robust style of writing in which sexual analogy plays a considerable part even on nonsexual matters, but although the origins of such developments within the Family such as the institution of plural wives, trial marriages, etc., can be accounted for partly in terms of Mo's own sexual appetites, again they provide no explanation for the distribution of sexual resources beyond the confines of the Family (Wallis 1978:72).

Reading this analysis in the early 1980s, I was struck by the way in which women were characterized as sexual capital, with no regard to the assumptions that underlie such interpretations nor to the effects of this objectification and exploitation on the women who were designated as "resources" in the religious community. The accounts of the individuals in my study provided a very different perspective on practices such as flirty fishing and suggested strongly that women's religious affiliation and experience had been ignored, silenced, or trivialized. I saw a need for an analysis that would situate religious experience and disillusionment within the framework of patriarchal charismatic structures. I thus began to investigate the effects of male power, both social and spiritual, on female devotees and to explore the interpersonal dynamics of commitment to spiritual authority. By contextualizing the socio-emotional dimensions of conversion within the structure of patriarchal religious movements, my work became interdisciplinary, drawing on the theoretical paradigms of both psychology and sociology.

Encounters with new religious movement research, such as the Children of God analysis, were pivotal in my development as a feminist scholar. At the time that my work first began to appear, the scholarship on the anti-cult movement was beginning to gain prominence. I found myself in the middle of a disciplinary war between psychologists who pathologized conversion and sociologists who were concerned with the demonization of nontraditional religious groups and the attending issues of religious freedom (Robbins and Anthony 1982). In this contentious battleground of religious studies, theories of brainwashing vied for prominence alongside social community models of religious commitment (Robbins and Anthony 1972; Verdier 1977; Conway and Siegelman 1978). My work, which explicitly challenged the brainwashing model, nevertheless was perceived as "anti-cult" because of its focus on the abuse of power by the religious leadership. Accordingly, as a young and outspoken feminist researcher in the sociology of religion, I had many obstacles to overcome: First, I was not a "pure" sociologist but one of those messy academics who refused to recognize or observe the boundaries between disciplines; second, I thought women were important subjects of research and sought to bring their experience to the discourse on new religious movements; and third, I insisted on raising the painful underside of commitment to charismatic groups — the violence and emotionally damaging aspects of patriarchal power relations.

The issues of power and violence that informed my early work are now recognized as important areas of study within new religious movement scholarship, particularly as the unraveling of the communities became apparent and the abuses self evident (Puttick 1997). When I first started out, however, my work was considered suspect and my feminist analysis a threat to the existing paradigms of religious conversion and disaffection. During my formative years as a gender scholar, I am not sure I would have succeeded without the support and encouragement of James Downton, my advisor at the University of Colorado, and Donald Capps who, as editor of the *Journal for the Scientific Study of Religion* in the early 1980s, believed in the value of my research and helped me to create an intellectual space where sociology and psychology could be brought together in a gendered understanding of religious commitment.

THE "SECOND WAVE" OF FEMINISM: FINDING THE ETHNIC SCHOLAR WITHIN MYSELF

Early on in my work on new religious communities, the significance of the charismatic leader emerged as an essential factor in both commitment to and disillusionment with alternative religious groups. As the research revealed the importance of strong emotional attachments in the development of religious commitment, another more troubling aspect of the teacher/follower relationship also became apparent, as the spiritual leader often assumed the role of an idealized father figure among the devotees. The parental dynamic evident within the groups had social as well as psychological implications that, for many of the women, mirrored pre-existing domineering and abusive relationships in the family of origin. The reproduction of varied forms of abuse — psychological, physical, and sexual — within the surrogate family structure of charismatic movements, led me to consider the effects of childhood abuse on the development of the self, a study that went far beyond the scope of religious conversion. For the next four years, I was immersed in a study of diverse forms of emotional and sexual violation and the effects of this violence on adolescent and adult women whose life choices and spiritual paths intersected with their abuse history.

An important finding of this research was the female child's identification with and emotional attachment to an abusive male caretaker. In an interesting parallel with the earlier study of charismatic leadership, my work focused on the significance of the father figure for the development of the female self within the context of family violence. This work led to two important findings on the role that religion plays in the abusive household and the importance of race and ethnicity in the formation of personality. With regard to the first finding, my study replicated other research on sexual abuse in religious families, confirming that abusive fathers frequently sanction their behavior through references to religious stories and texts and that, for the child, god as a punishing figure is often conflated with the father as a violent and punishing parent (Imbent and Jorker 1992). Secondly, my work elaborated the effects of racism and anti-semitism on victimized girls and women from African-American and Jewish families. Among incest survivors, disclosure of abuse was particularly problematic as revelations of family violence not only put the family at risk but the racial and ethnic community as well. Fears of racism and antisemitism thus were intertwined with the abused child's sense of responsibility both to the abuser and to the marginalized culture within which the violent family resided.

In what has become my "second wave" of feminist research, the finding on racism and antisemitism awoke the "ethnic" scholar within myself. The narratives of the respondents in the incest study made it painfully clear that Jewish ethnicity is far reaching and complicated in a society where assimilationism is the cultural norm and expectation. Under conditions of family violence, Jewish ethnicity adds a further source of shame and stress for those who are in the process of integrating the reality of abuse with the loss of the idealized father figure. While the struggle to heal has many dimensions and facets, Jewish victims of family violence, like daughters in African-American families, feel the need to protect the abuser, often explaining his violence through the lens of social injustice and persecution. As I came to understand the effects of ethnicity on the dynamics of family violence and disclosure, I turned to Freud and the controversy surrounding his early work on hysteria and childhood sexualization.

The story of Freud's reversal of his theory of sexual trauma is well known in the history of psychoanalysis (Masson 1984; Miller 1984; Rush 1980). In 1896, Freud presented a paper on the aetiology of hysteria to the Society of Psychiatry and Neurology in which he passionately put forward a theory of personality disorder that was grounded in his belief that hysteria in adulthood was linked to sexual abuse in childhood.

> I therefore put forward the thesis that at the bottom of every case of hysteria there are *one or more occurrences of premature sexual experience*, occurrences which belong to the earliest years of childhood but which can be reproduced through the work of psycho-analysis in spite of the

intervening decades. I believe that this is an important finding, the discovery of a caput Nili in neuropathology (1949:203).

Although Freud believed that his trauma theory made a revolutionary contribution to neurological studies, his paper received a chilly reception from the medical community. In the course of the next few years, he denounced his 1896 conclusions, maintaining that sexual abuse, as described by his patients, was just too prevalent to be real (Wolff 1988). In reversing his position, Freud constructed a theory of the female oedipal crisis in which sexual longing rather than sexual trauma was at the core of personality dysfunction. Prompted by the findings on ethnicity and race in my own study of incest, I became deeply interested in the relationship between Freud's shifting theoretical position and his religious/ethnic identity. I knew that many of Freud's patients were of Jewish background and I could not help but consider how Freud's social location as a Jew in an increasingly antisemitic society effected, consciously or unconsciously, the construction of a female oedipal drama wherein daughters rather than fathers became the perpetrators in fantasies of sexual longing. Sander Gilman (1993) has written extensively on the vilification of the Jew in turn of the century Austria, noting that in the formative years of psychoanalysis, this field of psychology was devalued as a "Jewish" science. It occurred to me that Freud may have feared that his theory of sexual trauma would reinforce the notion that Jewish families were indeed deviant and pathological, a fear that he may have internalized himself. Whether conscious and intentional or unconsciously protective, Freud's shift in thought pathologized girls and women, while obscuring the more painful truths of sexual violence that he once believed lay at the heart of his patients' psychoses.

As I became aware of the social context in which Freud did his work, of the prejudice he encountered and the images of Jewish inferiority that surrounded him, I began to see Freud through the eyes of a Jewish scholar and to consider the multiple social forces that influenced his scientific insights and his understanding of the human psyche. The work on ethnicity, first in *Victimized daughters* (1994) and then in *Religion, society and psychoanalysis* (1997), forced me to confront my own identity not only as a feminist researcher but as an academic whose values and worldview emerged out of my social location as a Jewish woman in an assimilationist culture. Looking back on my academic career, I find it interesting and somewhat indicative of my own acculturation, that while I had chosen the study of religion as my life's work, I had avoided those areas of research that were linked to my own ethnic and religious roots. Through Freud, I became aware of myself both as a gendered and ethnically situated scholar. During the time in which I was experiencing this shift in ethnic consciousness, crypto-Judaism was emerging as a unique form of cultural persistence in the southwest of the United States.[2] As I explored the possibility of researching this phenomenon, my father became gravely ill and the decision to pursue this work took on an intensely personal dimension.

Like the crypto-Jews, my father too had a "secret" Jewish identity. His mother and grandmother, my grandmother and great grandmother, were Sephardim, Jews of Spanish ancestry. My great grandmother, Tillie Canella, bore her Spanish surname until her death. Yet, because my father's father was of Austrian Jewish heritage, an Ashkenazic lineage that was considered of higher social status, my father's Sephardic Jewishness was rarely spoken of or acknowledged. Over the last decade, much has been written about the class and racial difference between Ashkenazic and Sephardic Jews (Crespin and Jacobus 1997; Matza 1997). This research affirmed what I had already begun to suspect, that my father's maternal Jewish ancestry had placed him on the margins of dominant Jewish culture and thus had been a source of secret shame.

As a child, I heard references to the Marranos, the hidden Jews of Spain. When my father spoke of these Jews it was in whispers. They were martyrs and apostates, heroes of the Inquisition and Jews that were not really Jews. It was only as my father neared death that he explicitly spoke of the Marranos as his, that is my, ancestors. He repeated what he knew about his mother's origins. My grandmother came from a long line of Spanish Jews. Her ancestors had been forcibly converted to Christianity and they lived in Spain and perhaps Portugal where they practiced Judaism secretly before taking refuge in the Ottoman empire where they openly became Jews once again. Much later my grandmother's family emigrated to Eastern Europe, eventually arriving in the United States at the turn of the century. As my ailing father spoke of this background, he had come to embrace his Marrano heritage and the Sephardic revivalism that had become part of contemporary Jewish-American culture. When I began the crypto-Jewish project, I therefore could not ignore the similarities that existed between the crypto-Jewish descendants and my own family. The descendants and I shared the same persecuted Spanish ancestors and the same hushed and secret Sephardic identity. They, like me, were in search of their Spanish-Jewish roots.

As I delved deeper into this phenomenon, I began to see parallels with the new religious movement and family violence projects, as themes of secrecy, fear, and authenticity lay at the core of each of these areas of study. Throughout my career, my research has focused on the conditions under which silence is broken

---

[2] Crypto-Judaism refers to a historical religious phenomenon that originated in medieval Spain in response to the forced conversion of Jews to Christianity. A portion of the forced converts, while publicly becoming Christian, privately maintained Jewish rituals, beliefs and practices, creating a hidden religious culture that today is known as crypto-Judaism. These so called secret Jews were also known as Marranos, a term that is rarely used now because of its derogatory connotations. Descendants of the crypto-Jews have been the subject of numerous contemporary studies, including my own current work in the southwest of the United States.

and hidden realities revealed. Because of the nature of my work, the credibility of the research population, whether they be disillusioned devotees, victimized daughters, or Latinas/os with Jewish ancestry, has been challenged and disputed. Beginning with the new religious movements study, my methodology has been scrutinized and my motives questioned. I have been accused of eschewing the principles of positivism to misrepresent alternative religious groups and male spiritual leaders and, more recently, to overstate the effects of religious perse-cution on the historical construction of crypto-Judaism. A decade ago, I was forced to defend myself against those who, having valid concerns for religious freedom, nonetheless ignored the power abuses in new religious movements. Today I find myself in conflict with apologists for the Inquisition and with scholars who question the survival of hidden forms of religious practice.

Yet the voices of the respondents are precisely what distinguish these research endeavors as feminist and authentic, as the narratives of the partici-pants give texture and meaning to the study of religion, gender, and ethnicity. Through the current project on crypto-Judaism, I have been made aware of the significant role that women play in cultural survival, particularly among populations that have been persecuted and colonized. I have come to a much greater understanding of how fear and ethnic anxiety are reproduced across generations of families with Jewish ancestry, and I have become much more conscious of the ways in which antisemitism informs the developing self. Lastly, and perhaps most painfully, I have come to understand the effects of internalized oppression on Jewish culture, how racism develops in response to concerns over assimilation and white privilege, and how difference within Jewish ethnicity can lead to the creation of ethnic hierarchies that privilege white European forms of Judaism and Jewish identity.

Through this work, I have entered the arena of contested identities that informs much of the contemporary literature on gender and ethnicity. I believe this is a vastly important area of research, as women in post-modern cultures negotiate the socio-political terrain of cultural preservation and ethnic loss. Following the completion of the crypto-Jewish project, I plan to expand my work to include a study of gender, identity, and cultural survival in post-Holocaust Europe. The Spanish Inquisition and the Holocaust represent two cataclysmic disruptions in the development and maintenance of Jewish tradi-tion, identity, and culture. Since I began the crypto-Jewish study , new research has emerged on patterns of cultural preservation and secrecy among first, second, and third generation Holocaust survivors living in Eastern Europe (Goldstein 1997). I intend to explore this response to political, religious, and social oppres-sion as it informs our understanding of the role that women play in resisting cultural annihilation and in preserving threatened ethnic identity. This field of inquiry will hopefully provide insight into the ways in which women contribute to the creation of culture under adverse social conditions and will therefore be applicable to the study of religion and culture from a global feminist perspective.

In extending my work on Jewish religion and ethnicity beyond the study of descendants of the Spanish crypto-Jews, I further embrace my identity as a Jewish feminist scholar whose gender and ethnicity together provide the intellectual and emotional lens through which I study, understand, and interpret social phenomenon.

REFERENCES

Christ, C., and J. Plaskow, eds. 1979. *Womanspirit rising: A feminist reader in religion*. San Francisco, CA: Harper and Row.

Conway, F., and J. Siegelman. 1978. *Snapping: The epidemic of sudden personality change*. New York: J.P. Lippencott.

Crespin, D.R., and S. Jacobus, eds. 1997-98. Sephardi and Mizrahi women write about their lives. *Bridges: A Journal for Jewish Feminist Studies and Our Friends* 7:5-116.

Culpepper, E. 1978. The spiritual movement of radical feminist consciousness. In *Understanding new religions*, edited by G. Baker and J. Needleman, 220-34. New York: Seabury Press.

Freud, S. 1949. The Aetiology of Hysteria. In *Collected papers, vol. I*, translated by J. Riviere, 191-213. London: The Hogarth Press.

Gilman. S. L. 1993. *Freud, race, and gender*. Princeton, NJ: Princeton University Press.

Goldstein. D. 1997. Re-Imagining the Jew in Hungary. In *Rethinking nationalism and ethnicity*, edited by H. Wicker, 193-210. New York: Oxford.

Imbent, A., and I. Jorker. 1992. *Christianity and incest*, translated by P. McVay. Minneapolis, MN: Fortress Press.

Jacobs, J. L. 1994. *Victimized daughters: Incest and the development of the female self*. New York: Routledge.

Jacobs, J. L., and D. Capps, eds. 1997. *Religion, society, and psychoanalysis: Readings in contemporary theory*. Boulder, Co: Westview Press.

Masson, J. M. 1984. *Assault on truth: Freud's suppression of the seduction theory*. New York: Farrar, Straus & Giroux.

Matza, D., ed. 1997. *Sephardic-American voices: Two hundred years of a literary agency*. Boston, MA: Brandeis University Press.

Miller. A. 1984. *Thou shall not be aware: Society's betrayal of the child*. New York: Farrar, Straus & Giroux.

Puttick, E. 1997. *Women in new religions: In search of community, sexuality, and spiritual power* . New York: St. Martin's Press.

Robbins, T., and D. Anthony. 1972. Getting straight with Meher Baba: A study of drug rehabilitation, mysticism, and post-adolescent role conflict. *Journal for the Scientific Study of Religion* 11:122-40.

———. 1982. Deprogramming, brainwashing, and the medicalization of religious groups. *Social Problems* 29:283-97.

Rush, F. 1980. *The best kept secrets: Sexual abuse of children*. Englewood Cliffs, NJ: Prentice Hall.

Verdier, P. 1977. *Brainwashing and the cults*. Hollywood, CA: Wilshire Books.

Wallis, R. 1978. Recruiting Christian manpower. *Society* 15:72-4.

Wolff, L. 1988. *Postcards from the end of the world: Child abuse in Freud's Vienna*. New York: Atheneum.

7

Women Clergy Research and the Sociology of Religion

Adair T. Lummis
Hartford Seminary

Paula D. Nesbitt
University of Denver

As two sociologists of religion having researched women clergy for much of our academic careers, we have discovered sometimes hauntingly similar themes in our research and results despite the very different methodologies we use. Adair Lummis, faculty associate for research at the Hartford Institute for Religion Research of Hartford Seminary, does full-time basic research supported by foundations and evaluative research sponsored by various religious organizations. Her research on women clergy relies primarily on survey and interview methodology. Paula Nesbitt is a sociologist and director of the Carl M. Williams Institute for Ethics and Values at the University of Denver. Her longitudinal database of clergy occupational biographies, constructed from denominational documents, is supplemented by interviews and participant observation. Our aim for this essay is to explore other mutual themes — about how gender-related inquiries, variables, and findings have challenged or transformed our own scholarly presuppositions, interests, questions for further scholarly discussion, and research direction. For comparative purposes, our substantively different perspectives and experiences require a format that allows our respective voices to be identified.

DEVELOPING AN INVOLVEMENT IN RESEARCH ON WOMEN CLERGY

We both became involved in studying the situation of women in the clergy as doctoral students. Our individual research interests in women entering the ordained ministry were confirmed after receiving our degrees, as sociologists employed in seminary environments. However, our history of involvement in research on women clergy is quite different, reflecting both our own social locations and the timing of our entry into the field.

Lummis: During graduate school at Columbia University, I was interested in the sociology of professions and professional socialization, but not the sociology of religion. However, in 1972–73, I was asked by Union Theological Seminary, NYC, to do research relevant to redesigning their M.Div. program. This was a wonderful, paid opportunity to study a professional school and professional socialization that the seminary agreed I could use for my dissertation. The early seventies were exciting and tumultuous years at Union Seminary. In contrast to previous decades, the Seminary's whole concept of its historic mission to train "scholar-pastors" was being challenged both by outside constituents in academic and church circles and by internal constituents. One of the most important internal constituents were women seminarians, who made up two-fifths of the 1973–74 entering M.Div. class. In the early seventies, women were generally beginning to enroll in M.Div. programs at liberal Protestant seminaries in greater numbers than ever before. Female seminarians at Union, supported by several faculty members, began demanding that this ecumenical seminary be far more active in helping women become pastors, and that "feminist" (and that term was much used) perspectives be included in both courses and community worship. I am sure I changed as much as any Union student in becoming *consciously* aware of some of what women faced in attempting to become ordained.

This awareness was broadened after getting my degree when I came to Hartford Seminary. In 1979, Jackson Carroll, Barbara Hargrove, and I began research, funded by the Ford Foundation, on the experiences of the first large wave of women M.Div. graduates who were also the first women pastors most members of their congregations had ever seen in their congregations or in their communities. This research eventuated in the 1983 book, *Women of the cloth: A new opportunity for churches.*

In the ensuing years, the experiences of ordained and lay women in the worship life and leadership of denominations and congregations continued to be a research focus both in my policy and action research projects (mainly for the Episcopal Church) and for two basic research studies, funded by the Lilly Endowment, which I conducted with other women scholars then at Hartford Seminary. The first of these latter projects, with Miriam Therese Winter and Allison Stokes, was based on lay, vowed, and clergy women respondents who subscribed to feminist journals or attended conferences at women's centers. In the resulting 1994 book *Defecting in place: Women claiming responsibility for their own spiritual lives,* we looked at the sources of support these women, holding a variety of feminist values, used for remaining in their congregations and trying to change these in accord with their beliefs concerning both the female aspects of God and explicitly including women in worship services and church leadership. The second study, begun in 1993, with Barbara Brown Zikmund and Patricia M.Y. Chang, and published in 1998 as *Clergy women: An uphill calling,* updates the *Women of the cloth* study and extends it to look at the current experiences of clergy women and men in fifteen denominations. This research involvement has been pivotal in sustaining my interest in the social and cultural factors affecting women and men in the church.

Nesbitt: While a doctoral student at Harvard during the mid-1980s, I was searching for a dissertation topic. I had done an analysis of occupational feminization in my former career, organizational communication, which helped me to raise comparative questions about women in the ministry and the occupational feminization process. Concurrently, while completing a Master of Divinity program at Harvard Divinity School, I noticed that women's increasing influx into seminary did not seem to be improving the situation for women once they were ordained and seeking placements. After reading *Women of the cloth* (Carroll, Hargrove, and Lummis 1983), I knew that the study of occupational feminization would be important to pursue.

However, I was also in the Episcopal ordination process. I chose to delay the decision about my ordination until after my dissertation research was completed, for methodological reasons and because I needed to seriously evaluate the insights I was gaining on the sociology of the church. From one of my professors, William Bainbridge, I adopted the research methodology of "intense ambivalence," and kept notes on my awareness, research tensions, and risks of being a semi-insider. The most challenging aspect of my research was obtaining data. After getting nowhere with various denominational officials once they realized I was interested in gender comparisons, I decided to use clergy occupational biographies taken from the published directories of two denominations, which were sufficient to construct a data base: the Episcopal Church and the Unitarian Universalist Association.

Following graduation, I continued, expanded, and deepened my research on women clergy. I also became ordained in my denomination. While the seminary environment facilitated my knowledge of critical issues facing religious organizations, their clergy, and laity, I also found my perspectives and findings to be more controversial than anticipated. Moving to the sociology department of a secular university environment, I have experienced a more objectified interest in my research. My clergy ties have allowed me access to some of the more candid positive and negative attitudes about women clergy, but I honestly cannot say that they have substantively affected my research. The very consistency of findings between Adair Lummis, who is a lay woman, and myself, suggest that my ordination itself is not a significantly contributing or confounding variable.

IMPORTANT AND SOMETIMES PERPLEXING
FINDINGS FROM OUR RESEARCH

In our research involving women clergy over the years, we have both become cognizant of major issues affecting ordained women, as well as some perplexing findings we are sometimes at a loss as to how best to interpret.

Lummis: One of the most important and perplexing areas of research has been what impact ordained women have had on pastoral ministry. Many of those surveyed expressed the hope that the more women entering the ordained ministry, the more clergy there will be who engage in democratic decision-making with lay persons, and the more clergy there will be who focus more on a ministry to those in need rather than on moving up the ministerial career ladder. This may be true to some extent. However, that does not mean the definition of what is most valued in a pastor has changed. Those clergy who pastor long hours with very modest remuneration in rural areas or inner city missions are unlikely to become senior clergy and denominational executives, *especially* if they are women. Among the clergy we surveyed in 1980 and in 1993, women are more likely than men to begin and remain rural pastors or assistants in the larger congregations. Yet until ordained women move into senior pastorates and leadership within their denominational structures, they are not in the position to make key decisions which can affect mission and ministry directions far outside the regions in which they serve. The glass ceiling definition of hiring committees for executive level ministerial positions as implicitly requiring a clergy man, is unlikely to become more permeable until ordained women are as fully employed in well-paying church positions as are ordained men. This may not be easy to accomplish even by the end of the next decade.

Nesbitt: In relation to occupational feminization, the work of Barbara Reskin and Patricia Roos (1987) had alerted me to the notion of a "tipping point," whereby the increasing occupational concentration of women leads to declining opportunity structures. In my data, a 20 percent female cohort concentration seemed to hold optimal prospects for gender parity, at least through entry and mid-level jobs. At about 30 percent female, job segregation and attainment differences by gender became prominent even at occupational entry, indicating that men's relative opportunities and attainment benefited from high concentrations of women. Since interviews with male denominational leaders do not indicate they are aware of this relationship, it is likely a byproduct of passive discrimination. Too often, women and men think that because women have a substantial presence in an occupation, parity has occurred. Lack thereof becomes perceived as the result of personal rather than structural reasons.

IMPACT OF OUR RESEARCH FINDINGS ON US AS RESEARCHERS

Although as social scientists we keep an appropriate measure of detached concern from our research findings, as humans we are not immune to being affected by what we have so learned in light of our own values and assumptions.

Lummis: There have been two areas of findings from our clergy studies at Hartford Seminary which have necessitated my doing some careful, often difficult, reflection. First, research I have done shows that those women with strong feminist beliefs in the female side of God and women's fitness for ministerial leadership tend to be more proactive than less feminist women. This stance has involved trying to effect systemic changes to improve career opportunities for themselves and other women, as well as in trying to obtain rights for marginalized groups they see as excluded from the church or unjustly treated by society. This finding appears in some aspects to bump against a second finding. The second finding is that women with very traditional views of God as Father and women's subservient role to men in church structures, can also be engaged in very effective ministry to those in their congregations and in efforts to help the needy in their surrounding communities.

A traumatic example of disjunction between my research and my value stance occurred when I found that the more strongly that clergy women endorsed feminist values of increasing women's presence and power in churches and using inclusive language in church services, the poorer their overall health (spiritual, physical, emotional, professional). Because I wanted empirical support for my belief that feminist clergy women are among the healthiest people on earth, I had difficulty with these findings but believe that they need to be reported.

Nesbitt: Three of my research findings have particularly affected my own insight. First is the observation of the subtle and sophisticated measures of social control that elites have employed, particularly the ways that "divide and conquer" have been used to erode women's consciousness-raising. In my book *Feminization of the clergy in America: Occupational and organizational perspectives* (1997), I write about ways that some elite men undermine women clergy who succeed too well, or who continue feminist change beyond the boundaries that such men think appropriate. Rather than lose public face as supporters of women clergy, more subtle tactics of behavioral control are employed, such as withholding information, giving double messages, or otherwise deliberately putting women in positions where either they are no longer a threat or they are likely to fail. Similarly, such elites may engage in "rule changing," whereby seemingly objective changes are made in church policy with inattention to the disparate impact on women clergy. Within the Episcopal Church, as well as other denominations, with the increasing pattern of congregations seeking to hire women appointed as interim rectors for the permanent rectorship came the "no succession" rules forbidding interim rectors to be hired permanently. However, it became apparent that such rules tended to be circumvented for men. Additionally the debate about reinstating the conscience clause, which would allow dioceses to refuse to ordain or recognize women clergy, has been resurrected. Second, my clergy data have shown me how important it is for women in both high and low-level positions to form strong alliances. Gender must be a greater interest than class or status if women are going to attain autonomy and authority similar to that of men. Women so easily find themselves pitted against one another, which effectively neutralizes efforts for change. The process is wearing for both traditionalist and feminist women, while men cautiously assume the role of spectator or disinterested party. Third, working longitudinally, I have clearly seen that social change is not a linear process. Rather, I like to think of it as "tidal," or in terms of life course research, "generational." Periods of retrograde can be necessary for social critique and corrective, as well as to provide space and time for social accommodation. Women who assume a linear process can become disillusioned when the tide turns, and their defection can short-circuit further social change.

These three findings have affected me as a researcher by pressing me to probe into social behavior. Personally, they have affected me with a deeper wariness. Additionally, the insights that my work have given me into social change processes are immensely helpful in coping with resistances to feminist and multicultural transformations within both religion and the academy. Overall, I have become a better analyst.

UNDERSTANDING FEMINISM AS BOTH
A CONCEPT AND METHODOLOGY

Whether or not feminist values are a central focus of our various research studies, these values underlie much of what clergy women do or what others fear clergy women may do. Through our research, we have both come to realize the complexity of what is termed "feminism," especially in the church. We vary in our perception of whether there is a "feminist" methodology.

Lummis: Beginning my research in this area in 1973, I benefited from reading some of the extensive literature then available on feminism. In the ensuing years, philosophical and sociological studies of the varieties of feminism have proliferated exponentially, as depicted by Walsh (1999). Varieties of feminism, some of which conflict strongly, have been intertwined in my research on women in the church and are a continuing focus of study.

Other than taking into account feminist orientations in developing research foci and questions, however, feminism has not influenced my research methods. This is because I do not accept the premise that "feminist" research methods exist. In other words, participant observation, depth interviewing, and survey research by telephone or mail are research methods which can be done well or poorly, which are appropriate or inappropriate for the investigation, but are not in essence more or less "feminist" as ways of doing research.

Nesbitt: In graduate school I was resistant to engaging the classics seriously, concerned over perpetuating androcentric presuppositions about the field. Similarly, I originally resisted quantitative methodology, perceiving it to be "unfeminist." Fortunately, a feminist scholar I respected urged me early in my research to make sure that I got "hard data." Studies relying on interviews were abundant. Statistics provided credibility with both the academy and denominational officials, which would be important if I wanted to place my work within the mainstream. That conversation forced me to consider the real objective of my research. Consequently, I decided that I needed to conduct my research in a format that would interact with the mainstream. My secondary agenda was missionary: to help break down the resistance to religion topics within other feminist sociological areas. Rather than "opting into" tradition, I have regarded my return to several of the theoretical and methodological tools equated with sociological tradition as a "bilingualism" that has sought to serve two different audiences. Additionally, traditional tools have been effective in helping to deconstruct male hegemony in both the church and the academy.

I do think there is a distinctly feminist perspective — one that uses women's experiences and concerns as a starting point, or treats them at parity with those of men. If women had developed the first wave of sociology of religion theory, notions of religious experience, of religiosity, of roles on the margin, of generational issues, and of small group processes, probably would have been much more fully developed initially, with less attention given to denominationalism. Further, I think that methodological tools would have been developed at a more sophisticated level for addressing these interests.

When a methodology only looks at what is there, or bases its findings on the mean, it reflects a picture of dominance; neither the outliers nor margins, nor subverted or repressed voices, are picked up. However, any theory or methodology that lends itself to use or adaptation to feminist issues can be considered part of the feminist research repertoire. Methodologies also can be developed that are distinctly feminist, where closer attention is given to what variance, outliers, and missing data might represent as an integral part of the analysis; where research instruments and tools are constructed to analyze relationships and multiple layers of meaning; where responses are systematically compared with other behavior for validity and reliability; and where research is done collaboratively.

IMPACT OF OUR RESEARCH ON SOCIAL CHANGE

As sociologists we are primarily interested in discovery and analysis through research. It is also true that we have feminist convictions, and would like our research findings to be used to strengthen the ministry of women in the church.

We have similar and also somewhat different perceptions of where social change will occur in the future for clergy women.

Lummis: In our research on clergy women at Hartford Seminary, we wanted the results to make some positive impact on the future of women in ministry. However, it is difficult for any researcher to know what impact their work actually has had on any group or structure, since we almost never do follow-up evaluation. For the research which resulted in *Women of the cloth* (1983), we met at various points during the project with leaders of the eight mainline Protestant denominations in this study, particularly the "women with portfolio," whose national church positions involved helping expedite the influx of newly ordained women into parish ministry. From these leaders, we learned how they had used our findings in designing programs and policies for clergy women in their denominations. By 1993, when we began the second clergy women study, national church bodies no longer had senior staff positions devoted to helping clergy women achieve parity with clergymen. Therefore, since our completed research reported in *Women clergy: An uphill calling* (1998), much of our knowledge of the impact of our recent research on clergy women has come from individual comments and queries made to my co-authors and me, particularly from numerous reporters across the United States who have requested comments and various statistical results. Paula Nesbitt's research has been quoted along with ours in many newspaper articles to underline the point that career opportunities for clergy women have not equalled those of clergy men. This public forum for our results may facilitate policy change.

Nesbitt: The assumption behind my work is that institutionalized religion, specifically mainline denominationalism in North America, still holds credence as a public legitimating voice for sociocultural values underlying gender relations in society. Women seeking elite positions in religious organizations have the potential to influence social change in ways that benefit women's interests. However, some women, for their own well-being, simply may need to "opt out" of traditional clergy work, out of the clergy itself, or out of the church. Women working in religiospiritual ways outside established institutions and ministerial roles potentially represent a highly creative — and radically transforming — trend in religiosity. "Secular spirituality" is descriptive of spirituality that is sufficiently inclusive to allow participation in ways similar to Bellah's notion of "civil religion" (cf., Bellah 1975). This secular spirituality is being infused into caring professions, businesses, and other traditionally nonreligious occupations and institutions, and shares a substantial overlap with feminist movements in presumptions of gender equality and intellectual diversity. The long-range social change potential of this trend is important for us to study.

Perhaps the most over-riding implication for social policy, however, is a false consciousness, among both women clergy and denominational leaders, that a liberal feminist agenda of equal opportunity and access has been completed merely because women are being ordained in growing, equal, or greater numbers than men. As decisions are made about changing how ministry is enacted within religious organizations, attention simply is not given to the potential disproportionate impact on women clergy. Consequently, systemic inequalities become perpetuated and exacerbated, as well as new ones created. However, in *Feminization of the clergy* I argued that backlash, although a defensive measure, nonetheless is a gauge of social change that has already occurred.

Lummis: I agree, some gains have been achieved. If women hadn't remained proactive, these gains would likely not have come about. Some clergy women have been too zealous in their pursuit of these equality issues, and this has lessened their effectiveness as ministers and as catalysts toward greater acceptance of women in ministry. Because of their efforts and encouragement, women have made gains, but there also have been losses. If we decrease our commitment, the losses may outweigh the gains.

I also have mixed feelings on whether women should work through traditional clergy career paths. However, this does raise a second question. Should women continue trying to involve the male establishment in understanding the issues, or have we exhausted this avenue and should now move forward with our own agenda? Some of the younger men understand. But some of the more senior researchers and clergy, both women and men, seem to have difficulty moving away from traditional "male-oriented" ways of thinking and knowing toward a more inclusive model.

Nesbitt: I have noticed that when a critical mass of women or gender-oriented papers appear at annual meetings, polarization tends to occur along gender lines. One might call it a "white male support group" phenomenon. Provided that it doesn't become a bastion of "female bashing," it can be a vital part of social change for those needing to regroup, or who need a bit more time and space. However, concurrently, I think that feminist scholars need to continue to seek ways to include established male researchers and clergy. Not only can we continue to learn from some of their insights, but after witnessing a hardened conservative Roman Catholic priest do a radical turnabout on the issue of women's ordination, I hesitate to write off anyone. I realize, however, that some women feel the need to do their own feminist scholarship irrespective of men. Both perspectives make for a healthily diverse feminism. Established women who have forgotten their feminist roots, as well as young women who are happy to benefit from the doors that have been opened by their predecessors, but who do not want to be associated with feminism, may be acting from a perspective of male dependency, either to hold onto their jobs or for scholarly esteem. Some simply have set other agendas for themselves. The ideological diversity can be a healthy part of feminist change, as long as the feminist movement doesn't have too many "free riders" (cf., Iannaccone 1994).

Lummis: Despite our recent studies and those of others on church members' response to actually having a women pastor, particularly by Lehman (1993) for Protestants and by Wallace (1992) for Catholics, there remain those, most often men, who still voice the inaccurate stereotypes such as, "if you have a woman pastor, all the men will leave the church and the congregation will decline." Neither have all our findings been deemed acceptable by clergy women. As illustration, in our fifteen denominational comparisons of ordained women and men, we found women are just as likely to be democratic or directive in their pastoral leadership as are clergy men. This finding was not well received by several groups of clergy women to whom it was presented, who resisted changing their belief that women clergy are on the whole more democratic pastoral leaders than are clergy men.

CONCLUDING REMARKS

Clergy women are becoming a more accepted presence. Although their presence in top church leadership positions is not comparable to clergy men, women are now senior pastors, as well as regional and national church executives. Further, these women leaders are reflective, caring as much for guiding a united, gender, and ethnically encompassing church into the 21st century, as they are in just getting clergy women into ministry positions or increasing the usage of inclusive language in church services. There may be parallels between the future for clergy women and for women in the sociology of religion.

As we move toward this future, one question is: should we try to follow men's model of sociology of religion as a discipline or set forth a new order? While women's interests and experience would lead to a somewhat different way of defining the discipline, our perspectives would be vulnerable to similar kinds of critique that feminists have levelled upon the male-dominant tradition. However, perspectives reacting to the established norms have a creative opportunity to surpass the limitations of the old order. To do this effectively, one must understand the old order's strengths as well as weaknesses. What "tradition" in our field does well is to analyze and explicate religious institutional relations of dominance and associated aspirations. This is an important part of the social environment because relations of dominance sooner or later affect all constituencies. The difference, however, is that there are many other social processes of equal or more concern to feminist scholarship that add just as much to the sociological picture. Feminists need to travel through the vortex of traditional paradigms on their scholarly journey toward a new order. The key is to not let one's creativity become lost in the vortex.

REFERENCES

Bellah, R. N. 1975. *The broken covenant: American civil religion in the time of trial.* New York: Seabury Press..

Carroll, J. W., B. Hargrove, and A. T. Lummis. *Women of the cloth: New opportunity for the churches*. San Francisco, CA: Harper & Row.

Iannaccone, L. R. 1994. Why strict churches are strong. *American Journal of Sociology* 99:1180-1211.

Lehman, E. 1993. *Gender and work: The case of the clergy*. Albany: State University of New York Press.

Nesbitt, P. D. 1997. *Feminization of the clergy in America: Occupational and organizational perspectives*. New York and Oxford: Oxford University Press.

Reskin, B. F., and P. A. Roos. 1987. Status hierarchies and sex segregation. In *Ingredients for women's employment policy*, edited by C. Bose and G. Spitze, 3-21. Albany: State University of New York Press.

Wallace, R. A. 1992. *They call her pastor*. Albany: State University of New York Press.

Walsh, M. P. 1999. *Feminism and the Christian tradition: An annotated bibliography and critical introduction to the literature*. Westport, CT: Greenwood Press.

Winter, M. T., A. T. Lummis, and Allison Stokes. 1994. *Defecting in place: Women claiming responsibility for their own spiritual lives*. New York: Crossroad.

Zikmund, B. B., A. T. Lummis, and P. M. Y. Chang. 1998. *Clergy women: An uphill calling*. Louisville, KY: Westminster John Knox Press.

8

Women's Spirituality Research: Doing Feminism

Tanice G. Foltz
Indiana University Northwest

I was first introduced to issues of gender, religion, and feminist research about 10 years ago, rather late in my career. Before that time I had been working on my dissertation research with a Hawaiian Kahuna's alternative healing group, one I characterized as a new religion. My graduate program at U.C. San Diego emphasized qualitative research methods, and so I engaged in participant-observation for over a year, conducted intensive in-depth interviews with the student apprentices, and took a life history of the Kahuna healer. Having immersed myself in the setting along with the students I learned to access altered states of consciousness to perceive and direct invisible "energy" *("ki")* for healing purposes.[1] This phenomenological research gave me an insider's understanding of the group's structure and dynamics, its rituals, its specialized use of language, and its worldview. My introduction to the alternative healing class was my first contact with the fascinating and rich area of the sociology of religion,[2] and this experience informed my decision to study a feminist, witches' coven.

After earning my doctorate in 1985, I relocated to Seal Beach and taught part-time at several campuses in the California State University system. In 1988 a Long Beach colleague, Wendy Lozano (now Griffin), invited me to accompany her to a witch-sponsored Spring Equinox ritual. At first I declined as I didn't consider witches to be serious, or perhaps I was somewhat afraid of what we might find. Shortly thereafter, I reconsidered out of curiosity as well as a desire to begin new research.

---

[1] The Kahuna called this process of directing energy *"ki* extension" and everything the class learned was related to this process.

[2] For early articles see "An Alternative Healing Group as a New Religious Form: The use of ritual in becoming a healing practitioner," pp. 144-155 in R.K. Jones, ed, *Sickness and Sectarianism.* Aldershot: Gower Publishing Co. Ltd., 1985 and "The Social Construction of Reality in Para-Religious Healing Groups." *Social Compass* 34: 4 (1987):397-413.

89

Wendy and I attended the event together and were introduced to the world of Dianic Witchcraft, a Craft tradition that is radical feminist, separatist, and political. Over the course of that evening, I could see the research potential offered by this unique, secretive, and "closed" group. What most interested me was the witches' focus on meditation and visualization, processes that were strikingly similar to those used by the Kahuna. While his methods had been oriented toward the physical/emotional healing of others, the witches were using them to do "magic" and to heal themselves from the wounds of the patriarchy. While driving home we recounted some of the evening's events, and the promise of the coven as a rich and intriguing setting for participant observation became clear. Although Wendy was not fully convinced, within a week she agreed and became instrumental in gaining us entree into the coven.

Since Wendy's previous social science research experience did not involve qualitative methods we discussed traditional ethnographic sources as well as my earlier fieldwork and came to the conclusion that a team research approach would be valuable. With her background in social science and gender and mine in deviance, new religions, and social psychology, we felt our combined perspectives would enhance our understanding and analysis. After gaining the witches' permission, we officially began our participant observation at the Summer Solstice ritual.

RELIGION, WITCHCRAFT, AND FEMINIST RESEARCH

Researching Dianic Witchcraft was my first "up close and personal" interface with radical feminism. Dianics emphasize women's oppression and point to the European witch burnings as a "women's holocaust," they glorify pre-Christian pagan women as wise women and healers, and they denounce injustices done to women in the name of patriarchy. Deviating significantly from any religious or spiritual group I had explored, Dianic Witchcraft centers on "the Goddess," alternately symbolizing Mother Earth/Nature, the Divine Feminine, Female Creatrix, the cyclical connections between women and nature, and the interconnectedness of all life (Starhawk 1979). Beyond their focus on the Goddess, Dianics consider themselves to be "radical feminist and politically on the fringe." They focus solely on the Goddess to the exclusion of the God, the covens are composed of women only, and their rituals deconstruct patriarchy while affirming womanhood.

The witches borrowed heavily from Starhawk, a psychologist and political witch who has written numerous books on the Craft.[3] Her ideas had inspired the coven sisters to make their decisions collectively, using feminist process, and they prided themselves on not having a high priestess who wielded more author-

---

[3] Two of Starhawk's important early works include *The spiral dance* (1979) and *Dreaming the dark* (1982).

ity than others. This was my first introduction to a non-hierarchal worldview put into practice, and it inspired me to investigate feminist research methods, which in many respects overlap with qualitative methods. Both value the researcher's personal experience as an integral part of methodology, both challenge the positivist ideal of "objectivity," and view the research process to be one of collaboration, and both emphasize that the research "subject" is not an "object" (Ellis and Bochner 1996; Jules-Rosette 1978; Reinharz 1983, 1992; Smith 1987). Further, researchers in both traditions are encouraged to use "critical subjectivity" or "self-reflexivity" in analyzing their role in the research process (Johnson 1975; Jules-Rosette 1975, 1978; Mies 1991).

What sets feminist methods apart is that women's lived experience is the center of inquiry (Reinharz 1983, 1992; Harding 1987) and consciousness-raising is a goal as well as a "methodological tool" (Cook and Fonow 1986; Fonow and Cook 1991). The positivist "objective" stance is not only challenged, but replaced with a value commitment to making women's voices heard, to deconstructing gendered power relations, and to empowering women (Smith 1987).

Our investigation of feminist methods led to a change in our methodological focus, which had been qualitative and humanist, but not feminist. During the course of the year-long study, Wendy and I made an effort to understand why these women identified themselves as "witches," what their training had been, the significance of separatist spiritual space, and how they incorporated their magical worldview into their daily lives. The research topic was a "natural" for engaged feminist methods. We strived for an egalitarian relationship with the witches, and through our social interactions in and out of the ritual setting, we grew to have compassion for these women of whom we had originally been afraid. We came to realize that they were important co-collaborators in the research process, and the extent of their collaboration depended on our willingness to view their beliefs and practices with open minds. We found that self-revealing throughout the research process enabled the witches to feel more comfortable and able to relate to us as women.[4] As a result they treated us as coven sisters without our ever having officially apprenticed.

Our participant observation in the witches' ceremonies, retreats, and other social events led us to experientially understand the potential of feminist spirituality for transforming, re-integrating, and healing women's identities (Jacobs 1990; Reinharz 1983). Some rituals involved enacting ancient myths from a feminist point of view, revering nature, and sacralizing women's bodies. Other rituals mourned women's abuse in patriarchal society, and the ceremonies cumulatively contributed to the women's sharing of experience, increasing self-

---

[4] We divided the interviews based on the witches' comfort level with each of us.

confidence, and bonding.[5] The phrase "the spiritual is political" (Spretnak 1982) took on new meaning as we observed the women using their spirituality to change their lives.

Similar to Karen McCarthy Brown's experience, our fieldwork took us out of the "compartmentalized context of academia" and allowed us to connect our selves with our work (Reinharz 1992:69). The witches' rituals involved making sacred commitments to one's self, the women's community, and the environment, and they emphasized the role of personal responsibility. Doing this fieldwork sensitized me to the consequences of my actions. For the first time ever I began recycling household refuse and collecting litter from public places such as the beach, which I continue today. I began integrating the witch research into my Gender Roles and Deviance classes and placed stronger emphasis on sexual politics and women's issues in all my courses. As we began to understand the power of religion in perpetuating gender inequality, Wendy's research focus changed from the family to gender and religion. Once extremely uncomfortable with the concept of the Goddess, I came to appreciate this symbol of women's dignity and divinity as a challenge to patriarchal religions. Our fieldwork with the witches had changed us dramatically as women and as researchers. Without intending to, we accomplished the threefold consciousness-raising goal of feminist research: we learned about the subject of Witchcraft, about conducting feminist research, and we learned a great deal about ourselves and each other (Reinharz 1992:194).

THE MIDWEST YEARS

Wendy and I had begun writing our first paper while I was still in California and we continued the writing process when I moved to Indiana in 1989. Upon reflection it seems that although our subject matter and methods were feminist, we as researchers had not yet explored feminist models of collaboration. Instead, we simply divided the responsibility and wrote different sections, mailing our revised contributions back and forth across the country. Eventually this process materialized into our first co-authored article, "Into the Darkness: An ethnographic study of Witchcraft and death" (Lozano and Foltz 1990).[6] Later we learned that this segmental approach was much easier than engaging in full

---

[5] For examples of such rituals, see Foltz and Griffin (1996).

[6] This article is among the first scholarly publications on feminist Witchcraft along with Mary Jo Neitz's work on Witchcraft ("In Goddess We Trust") and Janet Jacobs' work on Goddess ritual ("Women Centered Healing Rites"), both in T. Robbins and D. Anthony (eds.), *In gods we trust*, New Brunswick, N.J.: Transaction Books 1990. "Into the Darkness" is reprinted in N. Herman (ed.), *Deviance: A symbolic interactionist approach*. General Hall Publishing: Dix Hills, N.Y., 1997 and in R. Tewksbury and J. M. Miller (eds.), *Extreme methods: Innovative approaches to social science research*, Allyn and Bacon, forthcoming.

feminist collaboration, a challenge we struggled with for several years while working on our next paper.

My relocation to the Midwest brought new research challenges. I was eager to hear more women's voices to gauge the prevalence of women's spirituality outside of Southern California. At the behest of one of the California witches I began attending Midwestern women's music festivals, spirituality conferences, and pagan gatherings where feminist spirituality rituals were practiced. I interviewed Midwestern spiritual feminists in an effort to find out how these women became involved in such groups, to what extent they were involved, whether they were inspired to political action, and how they were employing their beliefs and practices in their lives.[7] In analyzing the data I became convinced that women were embracing Witchcraft and Goddess spirituality to heal their identities as female "others" in patriarchal society, and healing became the focus of my research.

Because my research topic was unique, I was often invited to give campus presentations. When approached to give a talk at the Newman Center's "Soup and Substance" program, I readily accepted. Upon my arrival, however, I was informed that a group of community women had surrounded the building earlier saying their rosaries, and that angry phone callers were demanding I not be allowed to speak. It seems they had the idea that (a) Witchcraft is Satan-worship and that (b) I was a Satan-worshiper coming to talk about my beliefs. They were wrong on both counts. Against the invisible backdrop of protest I gave my talk to a capacity audience and attempted to deconstruct the common myths about Witchcraft. Although the audience seemed sincerely interested and many people stayed afterward, the initial hubbub exemplified a "guilty by association" problem that field researchers often are confronted with, especially if they study marginalized or "deviant" groups. Coined "the contagion of stigma" by Kirby and Corzine (1981), field researchers must confront two separate issues: the first concerns predominant stereotypes of the group and the second issue is the assumption that researchers are members or "true believers." When the stereotypes are extremely negative the researcher is likely to carry a stigma, regardless of the reality of the situation. Clearly one of the reasons we do such research is to understand groups about which we know very little, and to shed some social scientific light on the subject. In this spirit, I do my best to continue the educational process beyond the classroom by participating in brown-bag luncheons and IUN's Seminar Day for high school students, hosting campus discussions, and making myself available to the IUN Speaker's Bureau.

---

[7] Finley (1991) found a relationship between women's spirituality and women's political activism.

FEMINIST COLLABORATION

In the early 1990s Wendy and I made several attempts to write our second article, which we agreed would focus on research methodology. Each time we began writing, it simply did not gel. At one point I even flew to California to write with her, but our efforts were in vain. Our lives were painfully out of sync; while Wendy was anxious to produce publications, I was dealing with a traumatic family situation that led to separation, change of residence, and eventual divorce. I was trying to keep my professional life together when I was asked to revise my doctoral dissertation for a monograph series on Cults and Non-conventional Religious Groups. At that time I shifted my focus from the spirituality research to immerse myself in writing *Kahuna Healer* (1994) and the methods paper went on the back burner for another year.

In 1995 word got around that a colleague was working on an edited volume about qualitative methodology and reflexivity issues. Wendy sent me a feminist dialogue piece that was alternative and intriguing. Prepared to try again, we decided to approach our writing from a fresh angle. Using our research experiences as primary data, we combed through our entire set of shared field notes and wrote about events that we had personally responded to, and which had in some cases led to "click" (turning point) experiences. We reflected on the research process, examined ourselves as subjects of study, and traced the transformations we experienced as researchers involved with the feminist witches' coven.

Acknowledging the researcher's part in the creation of social knowledge, we revealed how doing fieldwork in a feminist coven had affected our research, as well as our identities as women and researchers. Still untenured junior faculty, Wendy and I engaged in feminist collaboration using an experimental writing style, and later we interactively co-presented our paper at professional meetings. Even though colleagues commented that our work was "moving" and "courageous," senior faculty on my campus advised against including it in my Promotion and Tenure file. By the time I received P and T, our article, "She changes everything she touches: Ethnographic journeys of self-discovery" (Foltz and Griffin 1996) was published in Ellis and Bochner's anthology on alternative methods. This feminist collaboration completed our agreed upon work together and it served to deepen our relationship as scholars and friends.

GODDESS SPIRITUALITY, HEALING, AND RECOVERY FROM ALCOHOLISM

During my early years of data collection in the Midwest, I wrote about Witchcraft and its relationship to mental, physical, and spiritual healing, as well its use in healing relationships. At one point during the research process, I unexpectedly found a link between feminist spirituality and women's recovery from alcoholism. It was such a surprising finding that I re-interviewed some of the original participants and located several more, this time focusing on the spirituality-recovery linkage. My findings in this exploratory study resulted in the paper "Sober witches: Women, spirituality, and sobriety"[8] and provided a foundation for continued inquiry.

I questioned whether the spirituality-sobriety linkage was the result of self-selection in my snowball sampling or if such a relationship existed in a larger population of women alcoholics, and to this end I distributed a questionnaire at a Midwestern women's music festival.[9] Of the over 100 women who responded, more than 50 percent had been involved with feminist spirituality. Forty percent of this group indicated they had found Alcoholics Anonymous (AA) to be less than satisfactory in meeting their spiritual needs and women's "special needs" such as childhood sexual abuse, incest, rape, or physical abuse. Their responses suggest that feminist spirituality helped them to deal with painful intimate issues while boosting their self-confidence and helping them to reestablish trust and bonding with others — all factors related to sobriety maintenance.

I had planned to continue this line of research, but several family situations arose that set me back. My mother died unexpectedly in spring 1996, and shortly afterward my father was diagnosed with terminal cancer; he died within a year. Although I went on sabbatical in the fall to study women's spirituality in Australia, my research was cut short when my sister had to undergo emergency surgery. After staying by her side for nearly two months, I returned to my own home, depressed at her condition as well as the state of my unfinished research. At that point Wendy asked me to contribute a revised version of my alcohol recovery paper to her new book. Excited about the invitation and very aware of the tight deadline, I immediately became productive. My chapter, "Thriving, Not Simply Surviving: Goddess Spirituality and Women's Recovery from Alcoholism," combines findings from my qualitative study along with the survey research, and appears in her anthology Daughters of the Goddess (Griffin 2000). Delighted to be included in this innovative effort, I attended Wendy's book launch reception and afterward we reflected on our history of working together. Having moved in distinctively different directions,[10] we consider our previous collaboration invaluable to our growth as feminist researchers.

---

[8] I presented this article at professional forums in the US, Britain, and Australia. It has been published in *Diskus* Online at www.uni-marburg.fb03/religionswissenschaft/journal/diskus/

[9] I am indebted to the Association for the Sociology of Religion and the Fichter Research Grant Committee for awarding me the seed money ($1500) for this project.

[10] Wendy is interested in Goddess spirituality and death and women's bodies as sacred text. See Griffin, W. G. "The embodied goddess: Feminist witchcraft and female divinity," *Sociology of Religion*, Vol. 56(1):35-49, and "Crafting the boundaries: Goddess narrative as incantation," pp. 73-88 in *Daughters of the goddess*, Alta-Mira Press, 2000.

CURRENT WORK

At present my sights are set on pursuing the alcoholism research.[11] It appears that many women alcoholics never seek out AA or other recovery programs due to potential stigmatization, and those who attend AA Twelve Step meetings sometimes feel silenced by its traditional gender relations (Foltz 2000; Kruzicki 1987; Jarvis 1992). Their discomfort is reflected in recent research which suggests that a majority of alcoholic women have histories of childhood sexual or physical abuse (Miller, Downs, and Testa 1993), histories that are deemed "irrelevant" or inappropriate as topics of discussion in AA. Yet clearly these issues need to be addressed as part of women's recovery process. With the help of feminist colleagues, I plan to explore women's recovery in a number of women's religious or spiritually-oriented groups, including AA and other Twelve Step programs. It is my hope that this work will help to pinpoint the key variables in women's recovery — whether from alcoholism, narcotics addiction, eating disorders, sexual abuse, or from physical abuse — and will be applied to women's future health options.

FEMINIST RESEARCH AND SOCIAL ACTION

In an effort to make a difference in the lives of my students, I consciously use my teaching as the foundation of my activism. A feminist perspective has been integrated into the curriculum of each of my sociology classes, wherein the theme of gender inequality stands out. For example, in the deviance course we examine women's experience as "other" in all realms of life. Women and Crime deconstructs the myth of the violent woman offender, explores the criminalization of girls' and women's survival strategies, and examines various implications for women as prisoners and as workers within the system. Discouraging as this material may be, students exhibit increasing politicization and a desire to engage in activism over the course of the semester. As a result, many students ask to do internships in places such as battered women's shelters, a halfway house for crack-addicted women, the Sexual Assault or Domestic Violence Units of the local Prosecutor's Office, or centers for troubled teenagers. In these placements they get hands-on experience with real people who are living the social problems they have read about in class.

I have experienced great satisfaction teaching a course called Women, Religion, and Spirituality. After exploring creation myths and women's roles in traditional world religions and several new religions, we read feminist critiques and explore a variety of women's spirituality movements. I make a conscious effort to engage in "connected teaching," which involves students creating ques-

---

[11] I am most grateful for the encouraging and insightful comments of Wendy Griffin, Adair Lummis, Meredith McGuire, Mary Jo Neitz, Paula Nesbitt, and Michael York.

tions for discussion and offers a non-hierarchical seating arrangement to enhance the flow of communication. Students report that this method lessens the distance between professor and student and serves to elevate their feelings of worth and self confidence.

Another example of "doing feminism" is to mentor students and encourage them to present their papers in more formal venues. Each year I sponsor student participation in IUN's undergraduate Women's Studies "Celebrating Our Students" Spring Research Day, where students from all eight campuses gather together to give presentations, performances, and share their visual arts projects.

Throughout the years I have been very active in sponsoring campus activities that deal with the issue of violence against women. For instance in the early 1990s I hosted a campus discussion on date rape, and later moderated a panel of community experts who spoke about the issues of rape, battering, sexual harassment, and stalking. More recently, as part of my Women and Crime course, my students and I participated in an interactive self-defense workshop. As Chair of Women's Studies, I intend to push for women's support groups to assist students dealing with issues of incest, child sexual abuse, physical abuse, battering and sexual assault, and to facilitate the implementation of a campus-based self-defense class, all of which will serve our 70 percent women student population in their self-empowerment processes.

It is clear that my feminist spirituality research has transformed the way I view the world; it permeates my relationships and interactions, and shapes my professional goals as well as my personal dreams. In "doing feminism" every day, I strive to make intellectual, spiritual, and emotional connections that are empowering, and I honor the right we all should have to thrive in our lifetimes.

REFERENCES

Cook, J. A., and M. M. Fonow. 1986. Knowledge and women's issues: Epistemology and methodology in sociological research. *Sociological Inquiry* 56:2-29.

Ellis, C., and A. Bochner, eds. 1996. *Composing ethnography: Alternative forms of qualitative writing.* Thousand Oaks, CA: AltaMira Press.

Finley, N. J. 1991. Political activism and feminist spirituality. *Sociological Analysis* 52:349-362.

Foltz, T. G. 1979. Escort services: A middle class sex-for-money scene. *California Sociologist* 2:105-133.

———. 1994. *Kahuna healer: Learning to see with ki.* New York: Garland Publishers.

———. 2000. Thriving, not simply surviving: Goddess spirituality and women's recovery from alcoholism. In *Daughters of the Goddess: Studies in healing, identity, and empowerment,* edited by W. Griffin, 119-135. Thousand Oaks, CA: Alta Mira Press.

Foltz, T. G., with W. Griffin. 1996. "She changes everything she touches": Ethnographic journeys of self discovery. In *Composing ethnography,* edited by C. Ellis and A. Bochner, 301-329. Thousand Oaks, CA: AltaMira Press.

Fonow, M. M., and J. A. Cook 1991. Back to the future: A look at the second wave of feminist epistemology and methodology. In *Beyond Methodology: Feminist scholarship as lived research*, edited by M.M. Fonow and J.A. Cook, 1-15. Bloomington: Indiana University Press.

Harding, S. 1987. Is there a feminist method? In *Feminism and methodology*, edited by S. Harding, 1-14. Bloomington: Indiana University Press.

Jacobs, J. L. 1990. Woman-centered healing rites: a study of alienation and re-integration. In *In gods we trust*, edited by T. Robbins and D. Anthony, 373-383. New Brunswick, NJ: Transaction Publishers.

Jarvis, T. J. 1992. Implications of gender for alcohol treatment research: A quantitative and qualitative review. *British Journal of Addiction* 87:1249-1261.

Johnson, J. M. 1975. *Doing field research*. New York: Free Press.

Jules-Rosette, B. 1975. *African apostles*. Ithaca, NY: Cornell University Press.

———. 1978. The veil of objectivity: Prophecy, divination, and social inquiry. *American Anthropologist* 80:549-570.

Kirby, R., and J. Corzine. 1981. The contagion of stigma: Fieldwork among deviants. *Qualitative Sociology* 4:3-20.

Krieger, S. 1985. Beyond subjectivity: The use of the self in social science. *Qualitative Sociology* 8:309-324.

Kruzicki, J. 1987. Dispelling a myth: The facts about female alcoholics. *Corrections Today* 49:110-114.

Lozano, W., and T. Foltz. 1990. Into the darkness: An ethnographic study of witchcraft and death. *Qualitative Sociology* 13:211-224.

Mies, M. 1991. Women's research or feminist research?: The debate surrounding feminist science and methodology. In *Beyond methodology: Feminist scholarship as lived research*, edited by M. Fonow and J. Cook, 60-84. Bloomington: Indiana University Press.

Miller, B. A., W.R. Downs, and M. Testa. 1993. Interrelationships between victimization experiences and women's alcohol use. *Journal of Studies on Alcohol* (Supplement) 11:109-117.

Reinharz, S. 1983. Experiential analysis: A contribution to feminist research. In *Theories of women's studies*, edited by G. Bowles and R. Duelli-Klein, 162-91. London: Routledge, Kegan Paul.

———. 1992. *Feminist methods in social research*. New York: Oxford University Press.

Smith, D. 1987. Women's perspective as a radical critique of sociology. In *Feminism and methodology*, edited by S. Harding, 84-96. Bloomington: Indiana University Press.

Spretnak, C. 1982. *The politics of women's spirituality*. Garden City, NY: Doubleday.

Starhawk. 1979. *The spiral dance*. San Francisco, CA: Harper and Row.

———. 1982. *Dreaming the dark*. Boston, MA: Beacon Press.

9

Boundaries and Silences in a Post-Feminist Sociology

Penny Edgell Becker[*]

Cornell University

GROWING UP POST-FEMINIST

My encounter with sociology in general and the sociology of religion in particular began in college. In the 1980s, in that part of the Princeton sociology
department that I experienced directly, feminism was taken for granted in a way
that I encountered as positive. The push for more adequate categories of analysis
that capture the gendered nature of social life, including religious groups and
experiences, was part of the discourse of lectures and small-group discussions.
Functionalism, with its easy assumption that current social arrangements make a
larger whole that is if not "right" at least inevitable, had been replaced by a
conflict view of society, sensitive to power imbalances, multiple perspectives,
and opposing interests (Collins 1975).

And then I went to graduate school. The University of Chicago in the late
1980s and early 1990s was characterized by several inter-woven strands of post-
feminism. (A few of my friends insisted it was still pre-feminist, having been
skipped over by the revolution.) Post-feminism is also a way of taking feminism
for granted. But instead of asking feminist questions as a matter of course, post-
feminism incorporates some of the insights about social life and power arrangements of feminist discourse without making them an explicit focus of analysis
and debate. My encounter with post-feminism was less uniformly positive.

One strand of post-feminism is the idea that feminism as a social movement,
having pushed us towards a more egalitarian society (which is self-evidently a
good thing, and for which we are all of course grateful), is now essentially over,
and the radicalism associated with it has been appropriately replaced by appro-

[*] *The author thanks Kevin Christiano, Marin Clarkberg, Brad Wilcox, and various editors and reviewers for helpful comments on an earlier draft. She also thanks Nancy Ammerman and Phyllis Moen who, through informal conversations and their own work, have pushed her to re-examine her assumptions about the private nature of the family.*

aches to gender that seek consensus and value men's experiences. (We've grown; Deepak Chopra meet Robert Bly.) In learning how to do fieldwork, my insistence that gender be brought centrally into the account as a social location which constructs more than one "insider's view" was met with a reply of, "Isn't that just good fieldwork? Taking into account multiple points of view?" along with the assurance that, "Men have gender, too." In quantitative analysis, the equivalent was including sex as a standard variable in statistical analyses.

Another kind of post-feminism involved a building on and extending of the insights of an earlier generation of second-wave feminists. I remember Martin Riesebrodt's (1993) analysis of patriarchy as a personalistic system of power that constructs male-to-male, adult-to-child, and private-to-public status relations as well as those between men and women. And at a gender and society workshop I was pushed, for the first time, to go beyond the assumptions of a white, liberal, middle-class feminism to think more critically about other relationships of power.

However, I also remember classmates hostile to critiques of religious institutions as fundamentally patriarchal, who insisted that by making that critique I was devaluing women's own lived experiences of religion as meaningful. We had a hard time talking. They were drawing upon a neo-liberal view of agency, similar to that found in the work of people like Gary Becker and compatible with Coleman's view of the social actor,[1] which made no room for agency as socially constructed in a way that is simultaneously enabling and constraining. By definition, women participate in religious institutions because they want to do so, because their needs are met; criticizing these choices seems at best patronizing and at worst undemocratic. While I do believe we are all in one sense agents, I do not share the view of agency upon which they were basing their either/or dichotomy[2] (agents in this neo-liberal tradition either striding through history unencumbered or else being unjustly oppressed by any form of constraint — including the critiques of liberal feminist academics). In my "agency is more complicated than that" argument, they read a straightforward hegemony theory which was not there, thinking that I meant women suffered from some pernicious form of "false consciousness." We talked past each other, in part because I did not yet have the theoretical tools to make my case clearly.

---

[1] See pp. 28-29 in Coleman's *Foundations of social theory*, where actors are defined as one of the two elements of a social system — the other element being resources over which actors have control or in which they have an interest. Constraint is not part of the definition, and power is not a feature of the relationship between two actors or a property of the system, but resides within the actor (see pp. 132ff.). This is similar to a neoclassical economist's understanding of agency; when applied to relationships within the family, for example, such an approach leaves no room for a critical discussion of systematic imbalances of power that affect individuals' within-family negotiations (e.g., Becker 1981).

[2] For this contrasting view of agency see Giddens (1979).

In this kind of environment, post-feminism confronts the young feminist as something of a briar patch to be negotiated with care. How can one object to fieldwork practices that are more sensitive to point-of-view, to insiders and outsiders-within, without sounding churlish? Or object to including a variable for sex (plus interaction terms) in statistical models? These are not bad things to do, surely. They only frustrated me because I encountered them as boundaries; doing these things, it was implied, one could not reasonably be expected to go further or do more.

With a few exceptions, it was generally difficult to talk about how our theoretical apparatus might itself privilege a masculine — or masculinist — point of view, in an atmosphere where even James Coleman[3] could say to me, a first-year student, at a Friday post-colloquium reception, "I think all the interesting things have been written about gender, don't you? I mean, it's not really worth while spending time on gender as an entire category of analysis, there's nothing theoretically interesting there, don't you agree?" And it was hard to talk with other feminists who were only too ready to assume that anyone in the avowedly positivist sociology department must be tone-deaf to their concerns, if not downright hostile. My defense of some forms of positivism, along with my relatively feminine presentation of self (complete with jewelry and lipstick), did not allay their concerns.

My response to Professor Coleman at the reception set a pattern which I repeated more than once during graduate school. I was appalled, but smiled and said something polite about not really knowing enough yet to be sure, before I made my escape to think about things on my own. This is somewhat surprising to me still, since I soon obtained a well-deserved reputation within my cohort of being combative in seminars and colloquia. But I did not feel sure enough of my own feminism to fight over that. A pragmatist, I decided I could confront those questions as they arose in my own work, at my own pace.

The result was that, while I would readily self-identify as a feminist, I was not really sure what that meant for my work. I read quite a bit more feminist theory, incorporating that into my own knowledge framework under the larger category of critical theories.[4] In my dissertation, some feminist questions emerged. I explored how congregations negotiated with both a religious logic of caring for the believer and a religious logic of authoritative moral judgment in adjudicating conflicts over gender and sexuality (Becker 1997). An understanding of how congregations orient themselves differently to "the public" and "the private" informed my arguments about why group process and moral argu-

---

[3] A brilliant man, who actively fostered some forms of faculty and graduate student work on gender and status outcomes.

[4] That is, I understood feminism as one of many ways of making power central in the analysis of social life (cf., Agger 1998; Reinharz 1991).

ment play out differently across congregations (Becker 1998, 1999). But I did not use an explicit feminist theoretical framework to analyze where these different ideas — about private and public, about caring and authoritative judgment — originate. Nor did I explore their consequences for the gendering of local religious culture. I wrote a post-feminist dissertation and book, without giving it much thought, a boundary encountered in practice, perceived only after-the-fact.

RELIGION AND FAMILY

In designing a new project on the links between religion and family, based on surveys and fieldwork in four upstate New York communities, some questions flowed, quite literally, from my previous work in Oak Park. In 1993, when I asked pastors and lay leaders to name the most important issues they would confront over the next few years, the most common response by far had to do with changes in work and family. How were they going to restructure programming to include working women? How were they going to minister to single parents, divorced persons, those struggling with custody issues?

In a community dominated by young professionals, extended family networks were attenuated or missing for many. People were turning to congregations to be that extended family, a challenge congregations found variously invigorating or threatening, depending on their resources and sense of mission. One Reform Rabbi feared being swamped by "needy people" who would draw the congregation inward, toward members' own emotional healing, sapping their energy for outwardly-oriented peace and justice ministries. The pastor of the fundamentalist Baptist church saw new family needs as a natural extension of their prior forms of ministry, and enthusiastically organized fellowship groups for single parents and divorced persons. Pastors in upstate New York in 1999 ask similar questions, but they also employ a new discourse about the "time squeeze" effects on religious involvement, as they encounter families juggling competing work and activity schedules for parent(s) and children, including alternate-weekend custody arrangements and soccer leagues that hold practices on Sunday morning (Becker and Hofmeister 1999; Becker and Dhingra 2000).

In this new project, I have tried to push myself to ask how post-feminism has influenced both my own perspective and the previous sociological work on family and religion that I have encountered. I do not have the space here to render a complete account of that internal dialogue, nor do I have final answers to questions about the usefulness of a post-feminist interpretation of religion and family. But there are some silences that I have become determined to fill in, if I can, and sharing those may be useful to others thinking through similar issues.

Some of the silences in the literature on religion and family have to do with the way that these are both generally conceptualized as "private" institutions. Christiano's (2000) recent review shows that much of the religion-and-family literature takes for granted Berger's (1967) argument that religion has thrived in our society because of its mutually-reinforcing relationship with the family, both of which have been relegated, through modernization, to the private sphere of life (cf., Houseknecht and Pankhurst 2000). Religious institutions have powerful effects on marital formation and stability, on parenting behavior and the socialization of children, on marital satisfaction, on regulating sexual behavior to enforce norms of monogamous marriage, on married women's labor-force participation, and on the development of "familistic" ideologies (cf., Sherkat and Ellison 1999).

Religion is understood as private in the religion-and-family literature in several mutually reinforcing senses of that word. A voluntary institution, it is embraced or rejected by choice. It operates inside the heads of individuals, influencing individual behavior and beliefs. And it is private in that its most basic provenance is the sustenance of certain forms of what have traditionally been considered private life, the life of family and interpersonal relationships (Lasch 1991).

Sometimes, of course, religious groups "go public" in the form of inspiring publicly-visible utopian subcultures which critique the larger society, or in the form of religiously-based social movements on issues such as abortion and birth-control, or in the public statements of religious leaders about what constitutes a good family.[5] But this activity is generally seen as an attempt to impose upon public discourse values that originate in the private sphere. Even though the spheres are "bridged" by such activity, the idea that public and private are distinct, and that religion is most centrally located in the private, remains intact in such treatments.

In the sociology of religion, family is simply assumed to be private, although most acknowledge that families produce "public goods" in the form of well-socialized children, and through drawing parents into relationships that generate social capital (D'Antonio 1983, 1980; Sherkat and Ellison 1999; cf., Becker and Hofmeister 1999; Cherlin 1996; Parcel and Menaghan 1994). While I have always understood religious institutions as public, I did once share the assumption that the dividing line between "the private" and "the public" is coterminous with the boundary of the family.

So I was surprised when pastors from Unitarian and American Baptist churches, in an early focus group for the Religion and Family Project, talked about the public implications of organizing a church's ministry around a two-parent,

---

[5] For work that describes how religious groups "go public" on family issues, see Bellah, Madsen, Sullivan, Swindler, and Tipton (1991); Christiano (2000); Demerath and Williams (1992); Ginsburg (1998); Hunter (1991); and Luker (1984). Of course, outside of the religion-and-family literature, there are more general treatments of religion as a public institution; see for example Casanova (1994) or Marty (1997). For a critique of the Casanova thesis see Bruce (1996). For an explicit critique of Berger's thesis see Warner (1993); for an historical overview Warner (1999).

heterosexual family, of giving a religious imprimatur to norms of family practice that seem increasingly out of place in what Furstenberg (1999) has called the era of the post-modern family. Around 20 percent of the pastors in our clergy survey, almost all liberal Protestant, said they do not use the term "family ministry" at all because it is exclusionary, echoing in their open-ended responses some of the themes from the focus group. This led me to examine more seriously my assumptions about the "private" family, and I sought out colleagues to find out more about approaches to the family that take its "publicness" for granted.

It is not that the religion-and-family literature is wrong about the substance of the relationship between religion and family. But it does, I think, ignore the feminist understanding of the private *as political*, along with the feminist understanding of the family as itself a public institution, structured in large part by the state and the economy, mediating between individuals and a host of other institutions. As a result, a boundary is erected between sociologists of religion and others who study the family from a human development, feminist theory, or gender-and-work perspective. The latter, who usually have an explicit feminist commitment, often ignore religion entirely or assume that any religious influence on family life is harmful to women.[6]

This approach also leads to some silences within the sociology of religion, where attempts to answer feminist questions have a kind of awkwardness that comes from starting with a framework that accepts the family as a private realm of individual freedom and self-expression. Stacey and Gerard (1990) raise an oft-repeated question when they ask why any modern woman would embrace a conservative religion (specifically evangelical Protestantism). They answer it by arguing that these groups are not, in effect, as oppressive to women as feminists have supposed. Clearly beginning with a goal of making a straightforward critique of these groups as patriarchal, they end up making a sharp distinction between rhetoric and practice; in the latter, they find a kind of pragmatic egalitarianism ameliorating an ideology that symbolicly affirms male "headship" in the home.[7]

I always confront these studies with some surprise — not at the evangelicals, but at the feminists. I grew up in an evangelical Protestant environment, and am

---

[6] Recent reviews of literature in several areas of research on the family and family and work do not mention religion at all or treat it with only the briefest of passing mentions; see for example Cherlin (1996), and Shelton and John (1996) on the division of household labor, or Spain and Bianchi's (1996) review of recent research on changes in marriage, motherhood, and women's employment.

[7] For a recent review of the works on evangelical Protestantism see Christiano (1999) or Woodbury and Smith (1998), and for some good recent exemplars see Brasher (1998), Manning (1999), and Wilcox (1999). See Bendroth (1993), who argues that this characterization of conservative Protestants (as having symbolic male headship but practical equality) does not apply to fundamentalist Protestants, who are also quite patriarchal in practice. See McDannell (1995) for a distinction between a masculinist "official" Catholicism and a more home-centered and woman-friendly Catholic popular culture, and Davidman (1991) for an examination of women's roles in conservative Jewish groups.

not surprised to find that the very strong women I remember were not "oppressed" in the sense some scholars seem to expect them to have been. And I am sympathetic to arguments that not privileging long-term career attainment over family-oriented goals is not in itself anti-feminist, and that to equate the two bespeaks the biases of a white, middle-class feminism that may not apply so well across economic and ethnic boundaries. I am not calling for a feminist analysis of conservative religious groups that views the women within them as having no agency or as having a kind of "false consciousness" underlying their experiences of religion and family as satisfying and positively self-expressive.

But I do think there should be a place for feminist critiques of religion that are not apologetic, that treat issues of power relationships within marriage and family as inherently public, and that move past a pre-occupation with conservative religious subcultures to focus attention on a wider range of questions. Most self-confidently feminist treatments of religion and family have to do with issues like domestic violence, about which one expects no serious disagreement with the proposition that anything encouraging such behavior is bad (Nason-Clark 1997). But post-feminism has forsaken any theoretical ground from which to address issues of power in areas upon which there is no such taken-for-granted feminist consensus.

This way of thinking about the world sets boundaries around the kinds of questions that are even asked in the literature on religion and family, leading to systematic silences. Is the familism of mainstream (moderate and liberal) religious groups good for women, children, and men? It leads, research shows, to stable (even faithful) marriages, to satisfaction in family relationships, to well-adjusted children. In short, it is functional. Again, one would seem churlish to rail against such positive outcomes; it is rather like attacking kittens or chocolate, self-evident goods.

On the other hand, more women than men report feelings of stress and anxiety over balancing work and family, report high levels of guilt regarding their relationship with their children, and report having no free time for themselves. Does religiously-based familism support the idea that problems which arise in managing work and family life are disproportionately women's problems, for which they are responsible for providing private, individual-level solutions?[8] I never heard that question asked, perhaps because those doing the asking tend to come from within a mainstream religious tradition, or at least from the socio-economic location from which it springs. Hence, "the other" (evangelicals, fundamentalists, "marginal" religions[9]) prove sociologically interesting, while groups closer to home remain relatively unexamined.

---

[8] For a brief review see Becker and Moen (1999); Spain and Bianchi (1996) have a much longer review, as does Hays (1996).

[9] See Wessinger (1993).

There are other kinds of silences, too. In the face of new forms of family that are radically different than the male-breadwinner couple around which the last great religious expansion was built,[10] are churches of all kinds changing what they define as a good family? A few are questioning the idea of "the family" as the fundamental organizing unit of local ministry, and are including the rising numbers of long-term singles and childless persons in local religious life.[11] But these congregations exist in the same communities where other lay leaders and pastors still complain about the volunteer shortage that occurred, about 20 years ago now, when women "went to work;" these congregations are still struggling to find new forms of programming for women, children, and men that meet contemporary needs.

The huge variation in how congregational leaders think and talk about these issues has prompted me to ask how changes in men's and women's relationships at work, in the family, and in the church have transformed the gendering of local congregations. It has also made me question the link between changes in work and family and the proliferation of alternative religious spaces, including those like the Promise Keepers which focus explicitly on reclaiming a masculine Christianity. Has the "pluralization" of the family, as Furstenberg (1999) or Skolnick (1991) might call it, driven the pluralization of local religious cultures? Or the pluralization of commitment styles? Research has focused on the "gender gap" in women's and men's church attendance (Hertel 1995). But I want to ask if the *meaning* of religious involvement has changed for men and women after a period of rapid change in the work and family roles around which so many congregations have been organized for the past 45 years.

In raising these questions, I am only at the beginning of figuring out what a more positive kind of post-feminist account of religion and family might look like, and so have no compelling summary to offer, let alone a call to a specific research agenda. In my own work, I do want to take some feminist insights for granted. But I explicitly reject the idea that strong feminist critiques have had their day and must now give way gracefully to approaches that favor a consensual and functional, or even communitarian, interpretation of the good society. I am feeling more combative, or at least constructively critical, about theories that neatly divide society into a "public" and a "private" realm, while systematically devaluing those feminine things (religion, family) assigned to the private (cf., Warner 1999). I am not sure where it will lead, but it feels right to begin pushing back the boundaries of post-feminism by asking a different set of questions.

---

[10] For reviews see Warner (1962) or Ellwood (1997).

[11] For a review of the demographic changes see Treas (1999) or Furstenberg (1999). A few studies of individual congregations exist; for example, see Demmitt (1992) and Marler (1995).

REFERENCES

Agger, B. 1998. *Critical social theories: An introduction*. Boulder, Co: Westview Press.

Becker, G. 1981. *A treatise on the family*. Cambridge: Harvard University Press.

Becker, P. E. 1997. 'What is right?' 'What is caring?': Moral logics in local religious life. In *Contemporary American religion: An ethnographic reader*, edited by P. E. Becker and N. L. Eiesland, 121-145. Walnut Creek, CA: AltaMira (Sage).

————. 1998. Making inclusive communities: Congregations and the 'problem' of race. *Social Problems* 45(4):451-472.

————. 1999. *Congregations in conflict: Cultural models of local religious life*. New York: Cambridge University Press.

Becker, P. E., and H. Hofmeister. 1999. The time squeeze and access to social capital: Work and community involvement in upstate New York. Ithaca, NY: Cornell University, Bronfenbrenner Life Course Center Working Paper #99-13.

Becker, P. E., and P. Moen. 1999. Scaling back: Dual-earner couples' work-family strategies. *Journal of Marriage and the Family* November, 61:995-1007.

Becker, P. E., and P. Dhingra. 2000. Religious involvement and volunteering: Implications for civil society. Paper presented at the American Sociological Association Annual Meetings, Washington DC, August.

Bellah, R. N., R. Madsen, W. Sullivan, A. Swidler, and S. Tipton. 1991. *The good society*. New York: Alfred A. Knopf.

Bendroth, M. L. 1993. *Fundamentalism and gender, 1875 to the present*. New Haven: Yale University Press.

Brasher, B. 1998. *Godly women: Fundamentalism and female power*. New Brunswick, NJ: Rutgers University Press.

Bruce, S. 1996. *Religion in the modern world: From cathedrals to cults*. New York: Oxford University Press.

Casanova, J. 1994. *Public religions in the modern world*. Chicago: University of Chicago Press.

Cherlin, A. 1996. *Public and private families: An introduction*. New York: McGraw-Hill.

Christiano, K. 2000. Religion and family in modern American culture. In *Family, religion, and social change in diverse societies*, edited by S. K. Houseknecht and J. G. Pankhurst, 43-78. New York: Oxford University Press.

Coleman, J. 1990. *Foundations of social theory*. Cambridge: Harvard University Press.

Collins, R. with J. Annett. 1975. *Conflict sociology: Toward an explanatory science*. New York: Academic Press.

D'Antonio, W. 1983. Family life, religion, and societal values and structures. In *Families and religions: Conflict and change in modern society*, edited by W. D'Antonio and J. Aldous, 81-108. Beverly Hills, CA: Sage.

————. 1980. Family and religion: Exploring a changing relationship. *Journal for the Scientific Study of Religion* 19:89-104.

Davidman, L. 1991. *Tradition in a rootless world: Women turn to orthodox Judaism*. Berkeley: University of California Press.

Demereth, N. J. III, and R. H. Williams. 1992. *A bridging of faiths*. Princeton: Princeton University Press.

Demmitt, K. P. 1992. Loosening the ties that bind — the acommodatoin of dual-earner families in a conservative protestant church. *Review of Religious Research* 34(1):3-19.

Ellwood, R. S. 1997. *The fifties spiritual marketplace: American religion in a decade of conflict*. New Brunswick, NJ: Rutgers University Press.

Furstenberg, F. 1999. Family change and family diversity. In *Diversity and its discontents: Cultural conflict and common ground in contemporary American society*, edited by N. Smelser and J. Alexander, 147-166. Princeton: Princeton University Press.

Giddens, A. 1979. *Central problems in social theory: Action, structure, and contradiction in social analysis*. London: Macmillan.

Hays, S. 1996. *The cultural contradictions of motherhood*. New Haven, CT: Yale University Press.

Hertel, B. 1995. Work, family, and faith: Recent trends. In *Work, family, and religion in contemporary society*, edited by N. Ammerman and W. C. Roof, 81-122. New York: Routledge.

Hunter, J. D. 1991. *Culture wars: The struggle to define America*. New York: Basic Books.

Lasch, C. 1991. *The true and only heaven: Progress and its critics*. New York: Norton.

Luker, K. 1984. *Abortion and the politics of motherhood*. Berkeley: University of California Press.

Manning, C. 1999. *God gave us the right: Conservative catholic, evangelical protestant, and orthodox jewish women grapple with feminism*. New Brunswick, NJ: Rutgers University Press.

Marler, P. L. 1995. Lost in the fifties: The changing family and the nostalgic church. In *Work, family and religion in contemporary society*, edited by N. Ammerman and W. C. Roof, 23-60. New York: Routledge.

Marty, M. 1997. *The one and the many: America's struggle for the common good*. Cambridge, MA: Harvard University Press.

McDannell, C. 1995. *Material Christianity: Religion and popular culture in America*. New Haven: Yale University Press.

Nason-Clark, N. 1997. *The battered wife: How Christians confront family violence*. Louisville: Westminster John Knox Press.

Pankhurst, J. G., and S. H. Houseknecht. 2000. *Family, religion, and social change in diverse societies*. New York: Oxford University Press.

Parcel, T., and E. Menaghan. 1994. Early parental work, family social capital, and early childhood outcomes. *American Journal of Sociology* 99(4):972-1010.

Reinharz, S. 1991. *Feminist methods in social research*. New York: Oxford University Press.

Riesebrodt, M. 1993. Fundamentalism and the political mobilization of women. In *The political dimensions of religion*, edited by Said A. Arjomand, 243-71. Albany: SUNY Press.

Shelton, B. A., and D. John. 1996. The division of household labor. *Annual Review of Sociology* 22:299-322.

Sherkat, D., and C. Ellison. 1999. Recent developments and current controversies in the sociology of religion. *Annual Review of Sociology* 25:363-94.

Skolnick, A. 1991. *Embattled paradise: The American family in an age of uncertainty*. New York: Basic Books.

Spain, D., and S. Bianchi. 1996. *Balancing act: Motherhood, marriage, and employment among American women*. New York: Russell Sage Foundation.

Stacey, J., and S. Elizabeth Gerard. 1990. 'We are not doormats': The influence of feminism on contemporary evangelicals in the US. In *Uncertain terms: Negotiating gender in American culture*, edited by Ginsburg and Tsing, 98-117. Boston: Beacon Press.

Treas, J. 1999. Diversity in American families. In *A Nation Divided: Diversity, inequality, and community in American society*, edited by P. Moen, D. Dempster-McClain and H. Walker, 245-59.

Warner, R. S. 1993. Work in progress toward a new paradigm for the sociological study of religion in the United States. *American Journal of Sociology* 98(5):1044-1093.

———. 1999. Changes in the civic role of religion. In *Diversity and its discontents: Cultural conflict and common ground in contemporary American society*, edited by Smelser and Alexander, 229-243. Princeton: Princeton University Press.

Warner, W. L. 1962. *American life*. Chicago: University of Chicago Press.

Wessinger, C. 1993. *Womens' leadership in marginal religions*. Urbana: University of Illinois Press.

Wilcox, W. B. 1998. Conservative protestant childrearing: Authoritarian or authoritative? *American Sociological Review* 63(6):796-809.

Woodbury, R. D., and C. S. Smith. 1998. Fundamentalism *et al.*: Conservative protestants in America. *Annual Review of Sociology* 24:25-56.

10

Gender and Religious Work

Zoey A. Heyer-Gray
University of Missouri

I have a confession to make: I am still occasionally surprised to be studying the sociology of religion, in part because I came to the study of religion by way of one of those academic side roads (that, in my case, seems to have turned into at least a two-lane highway). As a feminist, and a secular and unchurched one at that, my sociological questions and interests have to do with gender and inequality, not, as a rule, religion. Eventually, however, after visiting churches week after week while doing field work for other peoples' research projects, I realized that my challenge would be to raise these same questions in the very particular and unique context in which I was (and would continue to be) immersed: the religious one. Gender thus became, for me, a "way into" the study of the sociology of religion — and it remains the thread that links my seemingly disparate research agendas.

As a feminist researcher I ask "where are the women?" And, indeed, Neitz asserts that this remains "a necessary question for sociologists who study religion"(1993:177). She also argues that "the feminist project of asking how any given experience is gendered also continues to be important. Individuals participate in religious organizations and movements as males and females" (p. 177). Individuals also do religious work as males and females. How, then, is religious work gendered? One of the aims of my current research is to begin to answer this question. Another is to begin to explore the kinds of religious work done by women. I ask "where are the women?" and find them all around — in the pews and the kitchens, at the altar and the organ, in the classrooms and the choir.

My research question — how is religious work gendered — is rather explicitly informed by feminist theory, in particular the feminist concerns with gender "as one of the primary axes around which social life is organized"(Kimmel 1993:vii) and with articulating the experiences of women in a meaningful way. More specifically, this research, like so much of the research done by feminists looking at women and work, is very much informed by Smith's work in *The everyday world as problematic* (1987), in particular her injunction to us to begin our inquiries with the individual's working knowledge of her everyday world (p. 154). This then becomes a point of entry for exploring the larger social and economic processes in which these everyday experiences are in fact embedded (p. 157, 170).

In elaborating her argument, Smith also calls for expanding the concept of work to a "more ample and generous form"(p. 165). She is not alone in doing so. Indeed, from the very earliest studies of housework (Benston 1969; Dalla Costa 1973; Oakley 1974), one of the arguments of feminist researchers has been that it is necessary to expand the concept of work beyond merely paid employment. Why? Because to equate "work" with paid employment effectively makes certain kinds of work, work that is often done by women as housewives and volunteers, "disappear from view"(Daniels 1987:403).

This brings us to another key feminist task: rendering visible those kinds of work that in fact sustain our everyday worlds — our households, our communities, our churches — but that are often difficult to "see" or discern, even occasionally for those who actually do the work.

These two key themes or tasks, expanding the concept of work beyond paid employment and making visible "invisible" work, inform much of the research on women's work. Authors in this area are desirous not only to analyze women's experiences in paid employment, but also to explore activities done by women that are frequently not considered "work" — at least not by the definition of work that equates it with paid employment — by either researchers or the women who do the work. Frequently this work is unpaid (e.g., DeVault 1991 on "feeding work" and di Leonardo 1987 on "kin work"), often it is "unseen" (e.g., Hochschild 1983 on "emotion work" and Daniels 1987 on "invisible work").

Of course, there is a third goal, as well, one that is sometimes more implicit than explicit, but nonetheless significant: to garner acknowledgement and respect for the work done by women, often in the hopes that this will lead to a more equitable and just sharing of these tasks. As Daniels notes: "Once we appreciate the significance of all the pieces of emotional and physical work that now do not receive the dignity and moral force of definition as work, we can regard the workers in a new light, appreciating both their efforts and their skills. . . . Serious attention to the importance of this work in the social construction of reality may make [the] sharing [of that work] seem more reasonable"(1987:413).

While I cast this research in a feminist theoretical framework and it is certainly informed by feminist research on women and work, it is also informed by research in another area of sociological investigation: the sociology of religion. This research is, in fact, an attempt to address particular gaps in this literature.

While much recent work in this field explores the experiences of female members of the clergy and the work that they do as pastors and formal leaders of the church (for example, Lawless 1988; Lehman 1993; Nesbitt 1997; Wallace 1991) there is comparatively less work being done that explores the work and experiences of lay women in the church.

Furthermore, much of the research that takes into consideration the experiences of lay women in the church is quantitative, explicating gender differences in religiosity (for example, DeVaus and McAllister 1987; Miller and Hoffman 1995; Thompson 1991). There is comparatively less qualitative work that explores the experiences of lay women in the church and even less that explores the work that they do (but see Pevey, Williams, and Ellison 1996; Gillespie 1992; Gilkes 1985 for some important and notable exceptions).

Although the aim of this note is to articulate the theoretical framework of this research and the ways in which it begins to address gaps in the existing sociological literature, I would like to conclude by offering some preliminary (and partial) answers to my research questions. The data discussed below is derived from fieldwork conducted at three different sites — a Catholic church, an independent Christian church, and a Southern Baptist church — over a period of several months.

WHAT KINDS OF RELIGIOUS WORK DO WOMEN DO?

At the Catholic church women performed a greater variety of tasks during the worship service than at either the Christian or the Baptist church. Women read, assisted in serving communion, brought the gifts to the altar, and read the prayers of the congregation — tasks that only men performed at the other two churches. Males would occasionally perform these tasks at the Catholic church, as well, but women were more likely to carry them out, and when a male did undertake one of these particular tasks he did so in tandem with a female partner — a wife, sister, or mother. The only task performed exclusively by men, aside from those performed by the priest himself, was the collection of the offering.

In contrast, women were much less visible at the Sunday morning worship services of the other two churches, despite the fact that over half of the people in the pews were women. Women did not perform any "public" roles in these churches other than singing and/or playing an instrument. Occasionally a woman might make an announcement or a prayer request, but they did not lead or say prayers during the worship service itself. Nor did they assist in the serving of the Lord's Supper or read from the Bible.

If we look beyond the Sunday morning worship service, however, we begin to notice that women at all three churches perform a similar array of tasks. Women teach Sunday school, clean the church, staff the nursery, and cook, serve, and clean up after church meals. The preschool at the Christian church — one of the church's key outreach efforts in the community — is, for example, staffed almost fully by women. And the Catholic church's annual fall spaghetti supper — an important fundraiser — is the responsibility of the church's women's group.

HOW IS RELIGIOUS WORK GENDERED?

Examining the tasks done by the women of these three churches — and noticing what men do and do not do — not only illuminates the kinds of work being done by women, but also begins to give us a sense of how religious work is gendered. Women are, overall, more likely to perform supporting rather than leading roles in the production of the Sunday morning worship service. They are also more likely to undertake the less public roles associated with the worship service (e.g., preparing the altar for the service, ironing the altar linens, etc.). At the same time they perform a whole array of tasks outside of the Sunday morning worship service — tasks that are key to sustaining the church and to giving church life its particular flavor.

My data at present offer only partial answers to the question of how religious work is gendered. The data also prompt a whole series of related questions. How, for example, does the gendering of religious work — and religious work itself — vary over time and by denomination? Answering these questions will not only give us a more complete understanding of gender and religious work, but also of the multitude of ways in which the religious or sacred is experienced in the day to day life of the women and men of the church. Indeed, the way in which something divine or sacred is in fact accomplished or captured by such a seemingly mundane process as "work" — and how this process is, in turn, gendered — remains to be explored.

REFERENCES

Benston, M. 1969. The political economy of women's liberation. *Monthly Review* 21:13-27.

Dalla Costa, M. 1973. Women and the subversion of community. *Radical America* 6:67-102.

Daniels, A. K. 1987. Invisible work. *Social Problems* 34:403-415.

DeVault, M. L. 1991. *Feeding the family: The social organization of caring as gendered work.* Chicago, IL: University of Chicago Press.

DeVaus, D., and I. McAllister. 1987. Gender differences in religion: A test of the structural location theory. *American Sociological Review* 52:472-481.

di Leonardo, M. 1987. The female world of cards and holidays: Women, families, and the work of kinship. *Signs: Journal of Women in Culture and Society* 12:440-453.

Gilkes, C. T. 1985. "Together and in harness:" Women's traditions in the Sanctified Church. *Signs: Journal of Women in Culture and Society* 10:678-699.

Gillespie, J. 1992. Gender and generations in congregations. In *Gender, spirituality, and commitment in an American mainline denomination,* edited by C. Prelinger, 167-221. New York and Oxford: Oxford University Press.

Hochschild, A. 1983. *The managed heart.* Berkeley: University of California Press.

Kimmel, M. S. 1993. Foreword. In *Men, work, and family,* edited by J. Hood, vii-viii. Newbury Park: Sage Publishing.

Lawless, E. J. 1988. *Handmaidens of the Lord: Pentecostal women preachers and traditional religion.* Philadelphia, PA: University of Philadelphia Press.

Lehman, E. C. 1993. *Gender and work: The case of the clergy.* Albany: State University of New York Press.

Miller, A., and J. Hoffman. 1995. Risk and religion: An explanation of gender differences in religiosity. *Journal for the Scientific Study of Religion* 34:63-75.

Neitz, M. J. 1993. Inequality and difference: Feminist research in the sociology of religion. In *A future for religion: New paradigms for social analysis,* edited by W. Swatos, 165-184. Beverly Hills, CA: Sage Publishing.

Nesbitt, P. D. 1997. *Feminization of the clergy in America: Occupational and organizational perspectives.* New York and Oxford: Oxford University Press.

Oakley, A. 1974. *The sociology of housework.* New York: Pantheon Books.

Pevey, C., C. L. Williams, and C. G. Ellison. 1996. Male god images: Lessons from a Southern Baptist ladies Bible class. *Qualitative Sociology* 19:173-193.

Smith, D. E. 1987. *The everyday world as problematic: A feminist sociology.* Boston, MA: Northeastern University Press.

Thompson, E. H. 1991. Beneath the status characteristic: Gender variations in religiousness. *Journal for the Scientific Study of Religion* 30:381-394.

Wallace, R. 1991. Women administrators of priestless parishes: Constraints and opportunities. *Review of Religious Research* 32:289-304.

11

Language, Gender, and Context in an Immigrant Ministry: New Spaces for the Pastor's Wife

Ann M. Detwiler-Breidenbach
University of Missouri - Columbia

It's Sunday morning in a tiny town, nestled in the Green Hills of northern Missouri, home of Premium Standard Farms, a center of corporate hog farming. As I walk around the deserted town square, I notice a storefront advertising the Calvary Chapel Bookstore. Through the windows I see Christian paraphernalia in both English and Spanish. On display are "Yo Quiero Jesus" bumperstickers and books in English by Chuck Smith, founder of Calvary Chapel. I take special note of the Santa Biblia/Holy Bible: a bilingual version of the Bible. One storefront, in particular, stands out. It is the local Mexican grocer, Mexico Lindo, an unusual site for northern Missouri. Its windows advertise Mexican foodstuffs, phone cards, and money grams. I'm in Florence, my site for the Missouri Rural Church Study.[1] In the evening, I will attend the Hispanic[2] service at the United Methodist Church. Walking around the quiet streets of downtown draws my attention to what the people who aren't attending the morning church services are doing . . . some, including myself, are apparently wandering aimlessly around the town square. My tablet, pen, and Bible are tools for the time I spend safely in the church pew. In the center of the square is the austere county

---

[1] This note is part of an ongoing ethnographic study, "Strategies of Well-Being: The Viability of the Rural Church in Changing Landscapes," funded by Lilly Endowment Inc. The Florence site was chosen as an opportunity to study the church's response to the shift in demographic composition prompted by the arrival of corporate agriculture.

My work has been influenced by the writings of Patricia Hill Collins (1991) and Dorothy Smith (1987) who have created a lens through which the location of the researcher and the intersection of race, class, and gender are brought to the foreground. I have also been influenced by the tradition of feminist methodology that emphasizes the giving of voice to women, especially those who are outside of the dominant power structure (Anderson *et al.* 1990).

[2] I use the terms "Hispanic" and "Anglo" as they reflect the local parlance of this community. I would like to thank Anthony M. Stevens-Arroyo and R. Stephen Warner for their contributions to my understanding of the need for sensitivity in the choice of terminology.

courthouse. It is surrounded by grass, sidewalks, and wooden benches. Many of the benches are occupied by men with skin the color of cinnamon, a shade not frequently seen in these parts until just recently. Being the single female strolling around the square, even in Levi's, makes me feel somewhat exposed. My light skin and brownish blonde hair may as well be glowing, considering how obviously different I believe I look to the others in town on this Sunday morning.

I imagine feeling different is not an uncommon feeling in this little town. In the last two years the demographic profile of Florence has shifted dramatically, thanks to the recruiting practices of the local corporate hog farm. Florence, described by a member of the local clergy as having been, "the whitest place I'd ever seen," changed shades seemingly overnight with the arrival of a Hispanic labor force.[3] A further characteristic of this new subgroup is its gender composition. The absence of women on the town square seems representative of the larger picture. One can only hope that the billboards, which greet visitors on the highway into town, are practicing truth in advertising as they claim to be "Missouri's Friendliest Community." Some of the local churches are attempting to live up to that statement.[4]

As I enter the church, walking toward me is a woman. Very openly and warmly, she extends her hand to me and says, "Hello, I'm Maria. My husband Arturo, and I — we're the pastors here." She welcomes me to the service. I take a place at the end of a pew, near the back. A group of men walk in to the sanctuary. Each shakes my hand as he walks by me on his way to a pew. Their hands are rough; handshakes are firm yet welcoming. Their smiles are engaging, even if somewhat shy. Then comes a man who seems different from those in the stream of handshakes. This man is somewhat better-dressed, and has an air of ease as he walks down the aisle, surveying the church like a conscientious host would survey his party to make sure his guests were all comfortable and enjoying themselves. Maria joins him and they come in my direction. Through Maria's translation between Spanish and English, she introduces us. This is Arturo, the other half of the pastoral team. Again, I am welcomed.

Arturo conducts the service alone. Maria is at the back of the sanctuary, running the sound system. The music seems to be a significant catalyst for the mood of the service. At one point during the two-hour service, Arturo decides that he wants to play a certain song, but Maria can't locate the CD. He has her run home and get it. Home, as it turns out, is just next door. She returns, and we

---

[3] Some estimates place the number of new residents at 500, a 25 percent increase over the original population.

[4] In this particular town, prior to November of 1998, there were 10 churches. Since then, at least 6 new ministries have sprouted up, each making an attempt to reach out to this new segment of the community. This is reminiscent of the church expansion during the immigration of the early part of the 20th century (Wuthnow 1988). These ministries are often supported structurally, by a larger, ongoing denomination, but have their own clergy, service time, and to a large degree, identity.

praise the Lord to a song about an eagle. I soon learn that this is a favorite symbol for Arturo in capturing the ecstasy of the relationship with God, con Dios.

Over the next several months I will witness Maria doing a number of tasks that don't fit into the conventional model for a pastor. Nor does she seem to fit a tidy profile of the indispensible, yet invisible (and inaudible), pastor's wife. As I witness Maria's role within this ministry, I see an individual who is needed by, yet never eclipsing, the official pastor, her husband. In public functions such as services and conference events, Arturo is the "pastor" of this ministry. Over time, however, I gain an awareness of the critical nature of Maria's position within the ministry, and the opportunity for having a voice that seems to come with being the *wife* of this particular pastor of this particular ministry.

Maria is the bilingual wife of a Spanish-speaking evangelical minister within an immigrant ministry. Like the evangelical women that Nancy Nason-Clark (1997) writes about, one might expect to find in Maria a submissive woman, relegated to the domain of the home. While she is a very nurturing individual with respect for her husband's work, "submissive" does not come to mind. Indeed, she is my point of entry into this ministry. From our first meeting Maria has introduced me to others as "our friend, Ana." After services, I sit with Maria in the parsonage kitchen, drinking coffee, while the men gather in the living-room, listening to music, loudly talking, and laughing. It is at Maria's kitchen table that I learn about the ministry. Though Maria often leaves her place at the kitchen table to make sure that the coffee cups of the men don't go empty, all the while she maintains a conversation with me about the ministry, new congregants who have arrived in Florence, word from those who have returned home, the latest interviews she and Arturo have done, and the latest round of affirmations about their ministry. Often her sentences about the ministry start with "We believe . . ." or "We do . . . ." She then modifies her words and says "Arturo believes . . ." or "Arturo does . . . ." In spite of this modification of subject, I experience this ministry as Maria's, too.

While I see Maria operating from a place of agency in her marriage, and in this ministry, my own experience with her husband contradicts this view. While he has literally welcomed me with open arms, he has seemed to place me in a specific female role of daughter and wife. Although he is less than 10 years older than me, he calls me "my hija — my daughter." Further, he has become preoccupied with finding me a husband. I wonder if this is an attempt to place me in a traditional female role which is familiar to him, taking me out of the role of the single female pursuing an education and a career. Though I have been able to get answers to my questions, I doubt that I'll be able to see this ministry directly through Arturo's eyes. While Maria has always been present, to translate, my sense is that "la estudiante" has been assigned to the pastor's wife. I decide to consider this as one more way Maria has voice for this ministry.

Indeed, Maria's facility with the dominant language places her in a strategic position in this ministry. "Maria is Arturo's connection to the white church," one resident describes their partnership. Arturo may give Maria the initial script in Spanish, but she breathes the life into it for the English-speaking audience, and it is to her they listen. This audience, not insignificantly, includes the District Conference, the governing body of this ministry.

Beyond language, by virtue of her gender, Maria can transform this ministry from a single man's ministry to a family ministry. According to the official "plan" for this ministry, authored by the Anglo church,[5] strong family ties is noted as being a trait of the Hispanic culture upon which the host church would like to capitalize. As wife and mother, Maria provides a public image of "family." She inherently places family at the forefront of this ministry, perhaps putting the long-term congregants at ease about sharing their sacred space with foreigners.

While, according to my interpretation, both language and gender are vehicles through which Maria is able to assert power and influence, context also seems critical. In this particular context, Maria participates in the intersection of two distinct cultures in the name of religion, which creates the opportunity for her to step out of a more traditional, supporting role of wife of an evangelical pastor. In past immigrations, it has been at this very intersection between culture and religion where change in the church has taken place as need dictated (Smith 1978). Maria is needed as the voice of this ministry. As one Anglo clergy member observed, "Arturo could not be Arturo without Maria." This ministry, led by a man in a predominantly male congregation, needs this woman's voice for legitimation.

Finally, Maria seems to be in the position of negotiating between the stated mission of this ministry as defined in the "plan," and the mission of her husband, who continues to focus energies on single men. One may assert that while Maria is tending to the public facet of the ministry, Arturo is free to tend to the souls of the single Hispanic laborer. One must ask, however, if Maria herself possibly has her own unstated mission for this ministry? As I read the words of Latina sociologist, Ana-Maria Diaz-Stevens, writing about Latina Catholicism, I begin to glimpse Maria and the position of agency and power from which I interpret her to be coming. Diaz-Stevens writes, ". . . upon closer examination of how power unfolds, it becomes clear that women exercise a productive function in religion; one that subverts and transforms social values" (1993:61). As the bridge between two cultures, with a voice in each, in Maria I see a woman of active faith who has the capability of using her place as a pastor's wife to step out of the

---

[5] This plan, the "United Methodist Hispanic Plan for North Central Missouri," authored by the governing body of the ministry, offers a rationale and vision for this ministry. It notes certain characteristics of this population on which to draw, such as "strong families." Further it states "The purpose of the United Methodist Church in the Hispanic plan for North Central Missouri is to . . . help assimilate Hispanic people into the established United Methodist Congregation . . . and into our culture."

definitions set forth by the evangelical Christian culture, and to be the author of her own profile of the pastor's wife.

REFERENCES

Anderson, K., S. Armitage, D. Jack, and J. Wittner. 1990. Beginning where we are: Feminist methodology in oral history. In *Feminist research methods: Exemplary readings in the social sciences*, edited by J.M. Nielsen, 94-112. Boulder, CO: Westview Press.

Collins, P. H. 1991. *Black feminist thought: Knowledge, consciousness, and the politics of empowerment.* New York: Routledge.

Diaz-Stevens, A. M. 1993. The saving grace: The matriarchal core of Latino Catholicism. *Latino Studies Journal* 4(3):60-78.

Nason-Clark, N. 1997. *The battered wife: How Christians confront family violence.* Louisville, KY: Westminster John Knox Press.

Peña, M., and L. M. Frehill. 1998. Latina religious practice: Analyzing cultural dimensions in measures of religiosity. *Journal for the Scientific Study of Religion* 37:620-635.

Smith, D. 1987. *The everyday world as problematic.* Boston, MA: Northeastern University Press.

Stevens-Arroyo, A. M. 1995. Discovering Latino religion. In *Discovering Latino religion: A comprehensive social science bibliography*, edited by A. M. Stevens-Arroyo and S. Pentoja, 13-40. New York: Bildner Center for Western Hemisphere Studies.

Warner, R. S. 1998. Immigration and religious communities in the United States. In *Gatherings in diaspora: Religious communities and the new immigration*, edited by R. S. Warner and J. G. Wittner, 3-34. Philadelphia, PA: Temple University Press.

Williams, R.B. 1988. *Religions of immigrants from India and Pakistan: New threads in the American tapestry.* New York: Cambridge University Press.

Wuthnow, R. 1988. *The restructuring of American religion.* Princeton, NJ: Princeton University Press.

12

A Clergywoman of the New Generation: Evolving Interpretations of Gender and Faith

Robin Albee
University of Missouri

This research note has unfolded within the context of a larger research study focused on examining rural churches.[1] As a researcher, I have a long-standing interest in rural and community issues. My work in the sociology of religion is a more recent pursuit, while the question of gender is something I have begun to address for the first time with this current project. This research note touches upon all three areas as seen through the eyes of Stephanie Howland, a female Methodist minister in rural Missouri. More accurately, this research note is a reflection on telling stories and the back and forth interpretive process between researcher and subject that this may involve.[2]

Stephanie is a minister to three small Methodist congregations in Millersburg, Missouri (pop. 257). Declining population as the predominant characteristic of this rural, agricultural part of the state, provides the context for small, often shrinking congregations with limited financial resources facing many rural ministers like Stephanie throughout the nation's heartland. In a sampling sense, Pastor Stephanie was of particular interest to our Rural Church project for two reasons. First, she is a student pastor with a three point ministerial charge — a strategy some denominations use when faced with communities that cannot afford to hire their own full-time pastor. Secondly, and more importantly in light

---

[1] Funded by a grant from Lilly Endowment Inc., Program on Religion, the Missouri Rural Church Project (officially titled "Strategies of Well-Being: The Viability of the Rural Church in Changing Landscapes) is a research project exploring the peculiar issues, strategies, and dynamics characterizing small churches in a selected number of Missouri townships.

[2] My primary research methods include participant observation, intensive interviewing, and document analysis. This approach is informed by interpretive and cultural frameworks useful for examining religious experience during times of change (which is one could argue most of the time), especially when these changes do not always fit into well established categories (Neitz 1990). This interpretive lens, combined with life history shaped narrative analysis, as theorized in recent feminist thinking (Anderson, Armitage, Jack, and Wittner 1990; Lawless 1991), is designed to reflexively look at the whole lives and listen to the whole voices of people as research subjects.

of the issues in this current research note, she is a woman, like an increasing proportion of new ministers.

Stephanie's small congregations are comprised of elderly people, with attendance ranging from about 8 to 22. She describes one open country church, the smallest one, as "a hospice situation." As a hospice worker, she says her main goal is help parishioners transition to a point where they will no longer be a congregation. The other open country church is, in Stephanie's words, "incredibly self-sufficient." She adds, with a laugh, that she sometimes thinks they would be just as happy to do their services themselves. She characterizes the third church, located within the town limits of Millersburg, as a formerly dying church that is now "poised for growth."

In addition to her three charges, Stephanie is also attending seminary full-time at a school of theology located about an hour away from Millersburg. "The position of a student pastor is a position advantageous to both student pastor and the congregational community," she explains.

> The churches, since they are small in membership, have never been able to afford a full-time pastor. At least not for probably the last 30 or 40 years. I don't remember when the last truly full-time pastor was. But at the least, in the recent past, they've had part-time local pastors that lived in the area, or retired pastors that worked part-time, or student pastors. They can't afford to pay not only the salary, but the benefits that the United Methodist Church would require, so it kind of works out well at the local level because they get a pastor, and it works out well for me because it's a good job and good experience.

Stephanie is young and energetic. The ministry is for her, like many of her seminary cohort, a second career. Stephanie's first career was as a corporate trainer for a major fast food franchise. Having interviewed many of the people in her congregations, I can say that she seems to be well liked and respected by all of her parishioners.

Going into the project, my assumption was that in some way, Stephanie's experience would be gendered. In our conversations, however, she rarely frames issues and problems in terms of gender and/or feminism. In terms of feminism, Stephanie's views were unclear to me. She says she does not identify herself as a feminist, although she quickly adds that she does not know what that term really means anymore. While not dismissing the role of gender, it is not in the foreground. Her relative youth (33 years old), she argues, is more of an issue than the fact that she is a woman. She does not believe that her gender affects how her congregation views her. "I don't think," she says, "that there is any huge gender inequity in my situation. There's nobody that's not coming to church because I'm a woman — at least not that I know of."

Recently, Stephanie and I sat down to discuss an article titled "Clergy-women of the pioneer generation: A longitudinal study" by Joy Charlton

(1997).[3] In this article, Charlton thoughtfully writes about the experiences of the first generation of women to attend seminary and enter the traditionally male profession of the ministry. For these "pioneer" clergywomen, gender and work combined in an altogether new fashion with particular, sometimes less than positive, consequences. Stephanie identified with several aspects of the article, but concluded that life for most beginning clergywomen is now different.[4] Her primary reaction to the text was that the author's interpretation was "too clinical" and perhaps "too sociological." In particular, she felt that the element of "faith" was missing. Talking about her own life, she explained, "But the fact is, everything I do is grounded in my faith in God and through Jesus Christ. You know that is the whole concept that is missing (in the article)."

In addition, I have given Stephanie samples of my own writings about her and the congregations that she serves. The hope is that this dialogic process would give Stephanie more voice in her own story and help create an understanding-centered dialogue. As with her comments regarding the Charlton article, Stephanie's primary reactions to my interpretations revolved around the issue of faith and its apparent invisibility in my writing. To illustrate, I've enclosed a portion of an earlier paper, followed by some of Stephanie's thought on what I've written.

> I recently helped out with the Millersburg Church's first ever Fall Harvest Sale fund-raiser. The dinner and auction were held in the unfinished, plyboard-covered sanctuary of the new church. There was a good turnout (150 people) and the church raised almost $6,000 to go towards the completion of the new church. The bulk of this money came from 14 panes of stained glass left over from the old church. Also on the auction block were arts and crafts, baked goods, leftover meat from the dinner (a big seller), and a large gas barbecue grill donated by the Wal-Mart in Macalister. The auctioneer was "a professional" from a neighboring community. Like most farm auctioneers I've seen, he was folksy, amiable, and inclined to telling jokes. He was decked out in his cowboy regalia and spoke (if that's what you call it when they launch into their stuttering, mile-a-minute auctioneer song) into a microphone

---

[3] Charlton adopts a theory by Everett Hughes (1945) on contradictions and dilemmas of status to explore the experiences of women in the 1970s representing the first real wave of women attending seminary and seeking ministerial work, particularly, in a congregational setting. Although smaller rural settings are not necessarily a central focus of her story, Charlton notes that smaller, and perhaps isolated, rural church ministries are quite often the first jobs that clergypeople receive.

[4] Charlton suggests that the women in her study adopted two different strategies in response to the contradiction of being a woman in a traditionally male field. One strategy was to foreground clergywomen's issues and seek redress where possible. Other women, however, chose to leave gender issues in the background and "get on with their jobs" (which they believed they could perform equally as well as men) and in the process de-emphasize "to the point of invisibility the contradiction" (Charlton 1997:604). One could suggest that Stephanie would fit into this latter category, although I would not make this assessment casually. Charlton explains these two strategies were not necessarily explanations offered by the women about themselves. Rather, more often, they were assessments of the experiences of other women in seminary. As research with Stephanie progresses, my hope is that she will feel comfortable to describe in her own words her reasons for backgrounding the context of gender, if in fact this is what she is doing.

connected to a hand held, lunch box sized amplifier. He was the entertainment for the afternoon.

Putting together this Harvest Sale was like throwing a big party and Pastor Stephanie was the host, uncertain really whether people were going to come to her big gala. She seemed anxious and emotional during the preparations leading up to the noon time start. Before people started arriving for the actual dinner and auction, she gathered together all those that had come beforehand to assist in the preparations. There were about eighteen of us: twelve people from the Church, an older couple from a neighboring church, Stephanie's parents visiting from Virginia, and myself. She talked about the hard work that everyone had put into this project, how the true church was represented by those people in the circle holding hands and not the physical structure that they were raising money to complete. Then she led the group in a closing prayer and blessed the food that had been prepared for the dinner. Throughout her little talk and closing prayer she seemed very emotional, although it was below the surface. With her red face and big glassy eyes, she looked liked a small child just on the verge of crying (Albee 2000:463-464).

In this passage, I focus on the emotion, and what I interpret to be the vulnerability of Stephanie as she attempts to initiate a meaningful and new ritual. Elsewhere in this particular chapter I talk about the event's larger purpose: to create a new annual ritual that will support congregational unity and reinvigorate a small, rural church that has witnessed a decade long tide of congregational decline.

While Stephanie agreed with much of my interpretation, she commented on how the crucial element of faith, again, seemed to be missing. She was surprised that I did not see God at work. "There was such a sense, not only at that moment, but through the whole project, that this was something that God was leading the congregation in. I truly felt that He was leading me in it and giving me the ability to lead it."

The research methodology for this project has, in effect, created a back and forth exchange between Stephanie and myself. A dialogue, based to an extent on differing interpretations and differing frames for reading situations, has emerged.

Stephanie's story about herself is a story of God. She is, by virtue of her call, doing what He wants her to do. Similarly, church and community activities such as the Harvest Sale are development projects with the Holy Spirit, not herself, as the primary change agent. Her faith, however, is not a simple brand of spiritual reductionism whereupon community and congregational problems can be explained by God. In her own personal and professional life as minister she talks about a number of challenges and issues with which she must deal. These include increasing congregational vitality, trying to deal with the isolation and loneliness of a rural area, reconciling what she learns in seminary with the more traditional views of her congregations (and, in several instances herself), and last but not least, worrying about how to pay off the high student debt she is accruing with the continuing prospect of a low minister's wage. And it is with faith, she emphasizes, that she is able to "look through whatever the difficulties are."

My story about Stephanie is — as I'm attempting to show — still evolving. This story would certainly include elements of her story and her words. Even though I cannot feel and sometimes cannot understand her strong faith, its centrality and the role it plays in how she sees the world has (through her words) become more clear. In my role as social scientist I am more inclined to see particular situations in terms of opportunity, constraint, and social structure. Thus, while Stephanie backgrounds the issue of gender, I would be more inclined to nudge it into the foreground.

Unlike many of the seminarians and clergywomen in Charlton's study of the pioneer generation, Stephanie grew up with women pastors in her church. She relates the story of how when she was a child her mother used to always tell her, "You would make such a wonderful minister's wife." Not to deny Stephanie's expression of God in her life, but a social scientific question would perhaps ask what her calling might have been had she not grown up with clergywomen and benefitted from the experiences of the pioneer generation.

I have not yet asked Stephanie what she thinks of my academic framing of this small story about her mother. It may be that none of the dialogues between researcher and subject, between Stephanie and myself, are ever satisfactorily resolved. My hope with this particular research project is that the process of creating space for an authentic subject voice and authentic dialogue will produce a better understanding of issues like gender . . . and now — well, faith.

REFERENCES

Albee, R. 2000. Clergywoman of the new generation: Evolving interpretations of gender and faith. *Sociology of Religion* 61(4):461-466.

Anderson, K., S. Armitage, D. Jack, and J. Wittner. 1990. Beginning where we are: Feminist methodology in oral history. In *Feminist research methods: Exemplary readings in the social sciences*, edited by J.M. Nielson, 94-112. Boulder, CO: Westview Press.

Charlton, J. 1997. Clergywomen of the pioneer generation: A longitudinal study. *Journal for the Scientific Study of Religion* 36:599-613.

Lawless, E. 1991. Women's life stories and reciprocal ethnography as feminist and emergent. *Journal of Folklore Research* 28:35-60.

Myerhoff, B. 1978. *Number our days.* New York: E.P. Dutton.

Neitz, M. J. 1990. Studying religion in the eighties. In *Symbolic interaction and cultural studies*, edited by H. S. Becker and M. M. McCall, 90-118. Chicago, IL: University of Chicago Press.

Nesbitt, P. D. 1997. *Feminization of clergy in America: Occupational and organizational perspectives.* New York: Oxford University Press.

Smith, D. 1987. *The everyday world as problematic.* Boston, MA: Northeastern University Press.

13

Mother Mary: The (Re)Construction of a Female Icon

Michelle Spencer-Arsenault
University of Waterloo

Though my research journey is very much in its infancy, writing this research note has allowed me to reflect on how my journey has evolved, as well as how my own personal experience, feminist ideology, and religious curiosity have shaped it. As I suspect it is with many scholars, researching gender and religion is in some measure a result of my own personal experiences. As a woman who was raised as a Catholic, I am well aware of some of the nuances of the Catholic church doctrine, especially as they relate to women. Although my experience ultimately led me away from this faith tradition, I have always remained intrigued by the fact that many women who experience the same questions, contradictions, and inconsistencies negotiate a place for themselves within the Catholic church. I think of women like my own mother whose life as a divorced mother of two certainly presents a contrast with the "ideal" Catholic woman. Yet her commitment to the Catholic church and her faith in it have been unwavering. If you ask my mother whether she believes in all the Church's teaching, I suspect that you would be told that you do not have to whole-heartedly embrace it all to be Catholic. She, like myriads of other women, has chosen to "defect in place" (Winter, Lummis, and Stokes 1994). Though her life and beliefs may not perfectly conform to Catholic teaching, her Catholic faith continues to hold a great deal of appeal and she therefore refuses to abandon it.

How do women, like my mother, negotiate between the reality of their own lives and the rhetoric of the Catholic church? In cases where contradictions arise, how do they deal with these differences in a way that allows them to continue to practice their faith? And what is the appeal that makes them want to? These were just some of the questions that I was entertaining when I first began graduate studies.

Probably a more important factor in carving out what I would later study, though, was some of my own early memories and impressions created by the Catholic church. Though I have distanced myself from Catholicism since leaving my mother's home, I can recall with amazing detail some of the powerful images that had been created for me by the Catholic church. I can still recall, for example, the huge statue of the Virgin Mary that stood in the corner of the corridor of the local convent where I attended my weekly catechism. I can still recall just how much the sisters loved Mary and how they tried to instill that same awe in every young girl. Similarly, I can still recall just how excited I was on the day of my first communion when I was given my own set of rosary beads. And finally, I can still recall hearing the voices of older Catholic women talking about the excitement of the May processions, or the importance of the many nights they knelt at chairs and recited the rosary with their families. These memories and the rituals they represent have been etched deep within my being.

In equally important ways, feminist wisdom has also played an important role in the way in which I have approached my research. Women scholars have partly paved the way for students studying the intersection of gender and religion. Not only have such scholars argued that religion plays an important role in creating and maintaining gender differences (McGuire 1997), their work has also consistently demonstrated that women can and often do experience religion quite differently than do their male counterparts. Similarly, such research has highlighted the fact that women are often active participants in negotiating and exercising their own agency in the context of patriarchal religious structures (Beaman 1999; Kauffman 1991). It is their work which has firmly established questions about the often taken for granted assumption that religious experience is homogeneous. These scholars note that the study of gender and religion challenges the notion that there is a "universal" religious experience (Jacobs 1998:206). Just as feminist scholarship has advanced our belief that social life is gendered, so too have feminist scholars of religion made us more aware of the gendered nature of religious experience and identity. At the same time, I have been challenged by feminist wisdom to regard women as more than just passive recipients in religious life, to recognize that they play an active role in selecting and appropriating the messages that they find meaningful in their lives.

So in many ways, my research journey began as a convergence between my memories from the past, the questions of my present, my commitment to studying women's lives, and my interest in how religion contributes to shaping these lives. My own personal experience suggested to me that religious teaching and the reality of everyday life may present women with a number of inconsistencies. Yet my own mother (and certainly many other women) appears as evidence that some women may be able to resolve these differences. Similarly, both my own experience and my training in the sociology of religion have taught me about the power and impact of religious ritual in creating systems of meaning. My graduate journey, then, began as a way for me to make sense of my own life as well as the lives of other women. The issue I sought to address was how Catholic women construct their lives as women of faith within a religious context where the model of Mary is held in high esteem, especially for Catholic women. What role does Catholic teaching on Mary have in the lives of contemporary Catholic women? Can an image that is so infused with patriarchal notions about women have any meaning for modern Catholic women? Does the image of a submissive, virgin mother have any appeal for women whose lives vary so dramatically from that model?

While Mary's image is one that is held as worthy of Catholic devotion in general, devotion to her has been especially emphasized for Catholic women (Daly 1975; Furlong 1991; Hamington 1995; Ranke-Heinemann 1991; Ruether 1979; Warner 1976). The Catholic church has created a whole tradition of devotion to Mary, emphasizing in particular her role as a virgin, mother *par excellence* and role model for Catholic women through her exercise of quiet obedience. Given these unique circumstances, I was intrigued to examine Catholic women's understanding of Marian teaching and the meaning they attach to it. Part of my research, then, sought to explore how ordinary Roman Catholic women in Eastern Canada *interpret* Marian teaching and *incorporate* it within their everyday lives as women. I found that for this sample of Catholic women, ritual played a considerable role in the importance they attribute to Mary's image.

MARY: AN IMAGE OF RITUALIZED AWE

Visualizing the Ritual

It was a bright and beautiful day in May. Each girl wore white and blue, and held mayflowers in her hand as she waited for the procession to begin. When the church bells began to toll, the girls started to walk through the streets toward the cathedral. Parents gathered at the curbside, snapping pictures as they watched their daughters pass by with such pride and purpose etched on their little faces. Onlookers stopped to see what was taking place. Mothers beamed as they recalled having taken part in this very exciting moment so many years ago in the presence of their own mothers. As the girls neared the church, each wished that she had been chosen to crown the Blessed Virgin with mayflowers. Upon entering the sanctuary, they processed down the aisle towards the altar, which was dimly lit with candles. In anticipation of the day's events, the statue of the Virgin had been placed in the center of the altar and each girl gazed upon her as if for the first time. Once the statue was crowned, the girls led the parish as they recited together "Hail Mary, full of grace. . . ."[1]

---

[1] This introduction was created by combining the stories told by numerous Catholic women about their participation in annual processions dedicated to the Virgin Mary when they were young girls.

Understanding Its Impact

For many Catholic women, images of Mary are inextricably linked to rituals such as the one described in the preceding paragraph. For them, it is their girl-hood memories of recitations of the rosary and their participation in annual May crownings that color their interpretations of Marian teaching. It is these vivid recollections of ritual which are an important source in underscoring the significance of Mary's image as a feminine icon, one that binds them to their church. Scores of sociologists have argued that rituals are an important source for reaffirming religious beliefs and a religious worldview in the everyday lives of believers (Ammerman 1987; Berger 1969; Greeley 1990; McGuire 1997). Interestingly, it was always with memories of rituals that these Roman Catholic women began to explain the importance with which they felt the Church regarded Mary — importance that seems to be woven into their own lives as well. These rituals, often performed with other women, whether they were class-mates taking part in May processions or their mothers leading recitations of the rosary, provide early impetus for the belief that Mary can have a special role in women's lives. In many ways, taking part in these rituals has provided a strong foundation from which the women in my study have come to interpret their roles as Catholic women in general, and Catholic mothers in particular. For these women, Mary's high esteem in the Catholic church is continuing evidence that women are highly regarded in the church, particularly for their roles as mothers and the vehicles through which the faith will be transmitted to their children. These rituals have inspired in many women a sense of awe. For, like Mary, Catholic women see their lives as mothers as an important part of their personal and spiritual fulfillment. Therefore although Mary is an object of ritualized awe, she can also be thought of as a "maternal friend" (Maeckelberghe 1989), someone who Roman Catholic women can relate to experientially. Mary had troubles during her life on earth, just as ordinary Catholic women exper-ience grief, loss, and anguish. In this sense, then, Mary is a bridge between this world and the world beyond. Her image provides both comfort and challenge in a world filled with disappointment, excitement, ambiguity, and despair.

REFERENCES

Ammerman, N. T. 1987. *Bible believers: Fundamentalists in the modern world.* New Brunswick, NJ: Rutgers University Press.

Beaman, L. G. 1999. *Shared beliefs, Different lives: Women's identities in evangelical context.* St. Louis, MO: Chalice Press.

Berger, P. L. 1969. *The sacred canopy: Elements of a sociological theory of religion.* New York: Anchor Books.

Daly, M. 1975. *The church and the second sex: With a new feminist postChristian Introduction by the author.* New York: Harper Colophon Books.

Furlong, M. 1991. *A dangerous delight: Women and power in the church.* London: SPCK.

Greeley, A. 1990. *The Catholic myth: The behavior and beliefs of American Catholics.* Toronto/New York: Collier Books MacMillan Publishing Company.

Hamington, M. 1995. *Hail Mary? The struggle for ultimate womanhood in Catholicism.* New York/London: Routledge.

Jacobs, J. L. 1998. Gender. In *Encyclopedia of religion and society,* edited by W. H. Swatos, Jr., 206. Walnut Creek: AltaMira Press.

Kauffman, D. R. 1991. *Rachel's daughters: Newly orthodox Jewish women.* New Brunswick, NJ: Rutgers University Press.

Maeckelberghe, E. 1989. Maternal friend or virgin mother. In *Concilium, motherhood: Experience, institution, theology,* edited by A. Carr and E. S. Fiorenza, 120-127. Edinburgh: T & T Clark.

McGuire, M. 1997. *Religion: The social context.* Fourth Edition. Belmont, CA: Wadsworth Publishing Company.

Ranke-Heinemann, U. 1991. *Eunuchs for the kingdom of heaven: Women, sexuality, and the Catholic church.* New York: Penguin Books.

Ruether, M. R. 1979. *Mary: The feminine face of the church.* London: SCM.

Warner, M. 1976. *Alone of all her sex: The myth and the cult of the Virgin Mary.* Great Britain: Pan Books.

Winter, M. T., A. Lummis, and A. Stokes. 1994. *Defecting in place: Women claiming responsibility for their own spiritual lives.* New York: Crossroad Publishing.

14

Personal Encounters with Sociology, Religion, and Issues of Gender

Lenora Sleep
University of New Brunswick

Within the hustle and bustle of contemporary life, times of personal reflection and assessment are rare. Whether it is when we learned to ride a bicycle on our own, the first time we felt love or hate, or when we first developed a passion for something like chocolate or jazz — these memories form part of our personal identity. As sociologists, our mandate is to reflect upon, analyze, and interpret social life, yet much of that time is spent trying to understand the life experiences of others rather than our own personal journeys. Yet, I am convinced that reflections upon our own history within the field can add great depth to our understanding and explanation of social life. In this research note, I will consider those intellectual and personal factors which have been critical in my development as a sociologist, and as a researcher of gender and religion.

GAINING THE SOCIOLOGICAL PERSPECTIVE

It was during my senior year of high school that I was first introduced to sociology, through exposure to theorists such as Comte, Weber, Durkheim, Goffman, and Marx, and this influenced my decision to continue studies within sociology at the university level. As I became more comfortable with the sociological perspective, I enjoyed learning of the diverse areas of the discipline (such as deviance, aging, social organization), and how the sociological lens could be applied to every aspect of life. The work of Nancy Nason-Clark played an important role in developing my interest within the sociology of religion. She challenged me to apply a sociological perspective to understand my own religious faith tradition, a lens through which to consider my life and the lives of others. Through this experience I caught a glimpse of what it was to be an 'outsider' within my own religious group. As I began conducting fieldwork I learned to listen as women shared personal religious experiences and then within my own mind I was bringing to life sociological concepts that I had encountered within the university environment. It was a strange yet exhilarating experience as I

133

translated religious language into evidence for sociological concepts. As well, I learned that there is a certain perspective that I bring to my research as a woman studying issues of gender. My identity as a Pentecostal and my experience as a woman shaped, in part, the sociological questions I was interested in answering through my research.

What I have learned over the years is the real danger of doing sociological research in any area where we, as social scientists, do not acknowledge and reflect upon our own biases before going into the field. As I familiarize myself with literature within the discipline, I note how rarely the relationship between the subject matter and the researcher is addressed within sociological studies. Yet, I believe it is a critical part of the story left untold — a part from which social scientists can gain knowledge and a clearer depiction of social life.

THE RESEARCH JOURNEY

As I continued on with graduate studies, I became increasingly interested in the impact of modernity upon religious life, especially those faith traditions which were conservative in nature. Donald Kraybill's study of the Amish brought to life the process of negotiation that conservative faith communities often endure in order to contend with contemporary culture.[1] Much like the Amish within Lancaster County, research findings revealed that the Pentecostal faith tradition had performed some boundary maintenance to include certain aspects of modern day society.[2] Yet, critical importance was placed also on being separated from those outside the fold.

My personal experiences with the Pentecostal faith community revealed a similar story. There were two central things that I learned being raised in a Pentecostal home. First, the Pentecostal church plays an all-encompassing role in the everyday life of its families. My sister and I played with only church friends, we were a part of many church-related weekday activities; we went to church twice on Sundays; we visited other Pentecostal homes with our parents; and we were enrolled in Pentecostal schools.

Secondly, within the Pentecostal faith tradition there is a tremendous emphasis placed on being set apart from "the world," sheep from goats. My parents, as well as our pastors, always spoke of how bad the world was getting and how hard it was to raise children in the day in which we lived. They sheltered us from secular music, were selective of our friends, monitored our television programs, and continuously educated us in all the dangers we would face growing up in a "sin-sick" world. In their opinion, things were either worldly or

---

[1] See D. Kraybill (1989), *The riddle of the Amish*. London: The Johns Hopkins University Press.

[2] See E. Lawless (1988), *Handmaidens of the Lord: Pentecostal women preachers and traditional religion*. Philadelphia: University of Pennsylvania Press.

godly, and as a result, they constantly tried to alleviate or minimize any outside influences upon our lives. As a child, the "do's and don'ts" implicit within my parents' worldview became the essence of my religious experience. Much to my parents' disappointment, the majority of my teenage years were spent experimenting with the "don'ts" from which they had so earnestly tried to protect me.

It was not until three years ago that I returned to my faith community and began to interpret my past association with the Pentecostal tradition as positive. As a result of my life narrative, I wanted to examine how others, particularly women, make sense of their own decisions and beliefs in light of church messages received from the time of their youth. Issues of paid employment and issues of family conflict were particular areas that I decided to address within my research on the Pentecostal family. I wondered if other Pentecostal women's life experiences with work and family life were also conflicting with church messages, and if so, how these women dealt with these discrepancies.

My interest in family conflict was largely a result of my work as a research assistant with the Religion and Violence Research Team, associated with the Muriel McQueen Fergusson Centre for Family Violence, on projects investigating abuse and faith communities.[3] It was not until my involvement with this team that I was exposed to the power of sociological research in bringing about social change.

DISCOVERY OF NUGGETS IN THE RESEARCH FIELD

For the remainder of this research note, I would like to highlight some of the "nuggets" that I have discovered in my adventures in field research, involving a case study of a small urban church located within Atlantic Canada. The triangulated research was conducted in three stages: participant observation and the collection of church literature; the administration of a church family survey to all congregation members aged eighteen and over present on a Sunday morning; and in-depth interviews with a small sample of Pentecostal wives. These nuggets relate to the process of research rather than results of fieldwork.

My first "nugget," or discovery, was a realization of the importance of the social context within field research. Through triangulation of research methods, I was able to contextualize the life stories of the women I interviewed, by reference to congregational data and participant observation in the field. One example: the senior minister of this particular faith community did not publicly declare (through sermons) the importance of the traditional family ideal, and did not personally maintain the traditional family ideal within his own family,

---

and this was an important insight from the field that helped me interpret church women's discourse within the interview setting.

Secondly, I have gained a true understanding of the importance of listening and hearing women's voices to understand the power of religion. Religious experiences, through history, have been predominantly told by men and about men, and almost never related by women or children. As women's perspectives and experiences are revealed, it is easy to understand that for women, the journey of faith is unique and must be treated accordingly. The use of loosely structured interviews within my own research allowed me to uncover issues and concerns that were significant to these Pentecostal women — concerns that could not have been conveyed by men of faith, or on a survey instrument.

Another important lesson that I learned in the field was to appreciate the complexity of women's accounts. Many opposing messages were given within each individual interview. At first, during my data analysis, I was tempted to overlook the discrepancies within the story of each woman to bring clarity to the presentation of my research findings. Yet as I explored further the inconsistencies within the interviews, I realized that these discrepancies were critical, a vital part of women's journeys in faith. These discrepancies ultimately reflected the process through which women were engaged in coming to terms with church messages and their everyday life experiences, and in fact, the interview itself aided that internal dialogue both within me, the researcher, and within the lives of the women I was interviewing. Although some of these women would express their wholehearted support of the traditional family form, their experiences and explanations of their own personal journeys with paid employment revealed another part of the story — what was so clear in rhetoric was obscure in practice. Through this experience I realized how life histories can often be more telling than religious rhetoric.

A further critical finding that the interviews revealed was how a personal relationship with the divine provides a bridge to fill the gap between religious teachings and life experiences within the Pentecostal tradition. When women of faith explained their involvement with the full-time labor force, they focused on the importance of God's will for their lives (revealed through prayer and Bible study) rather than on religious teachings. Other researchers of conservative Protestant faith communities, such as Susan Rose and Brenda Brasher, also reveal the significance of a personal relationship with God in offering women from conservative faith traditions a source of power, freedom, and justification in the midst of a patriarchal environment.[4]

The final nugget is the importance of researcher perspective. Ultimately, I learned the centrality of asking the question: From what perspective am I seeing

---

[4] See B. Brasher (1998), *Godly women: Fundamentalism and female power*. New Brunswick, NJ: Rutgers University Press and S. Rose (1987), "The negotiation of gender in a charismatic community." *Sociological Analysis* 48:245-258.

the lives of women of faith? It became obvious to me that I could have walked away from my research on Pentecostal family life with two very different viewpoints. I could have seen the glass as half empty — that these Pentecostal women were living restrictive lives within a patriarchal system. Half of the women were homemakers, spending their days changing dirty diapers and vacuuming, while the other half were working a 'double shift' and experiencing guilt for slipping in their roles as godly mothers and wives. On the other hand, I could have portrayed the glass as half full — that these Pentecostal women were active players who weighed the costs of working in full-time paid employment, and chose to remain home because it was the most appealing option. These women controlled the affairs of the home and were unwilling to relinquish their power or influence over home-life. Essentially, what I learned through this research process is to be open to multiple interpretations of the data. I have found that trying to see women of faith from many perspectives provides a deeper understanding of the complexity of their stories, and the social world at large. It is my hope, with the valuable insights that I have gained in the field, that I will be able to contribute further to our growing understanding of issues of gender and faith through future research endeavors.

About the Contributors

Robin Albee completed his MA in rural sociology at the University of Missouri in 1997. He has been engaged in ethnographic research on social movements and cultural changes in rural communities. This is reflected in his MA thesis, "Exotic, or wild: Contested constructions of free-roaming horses in the Missouri Ozarks." He is also coauthor on the study, "New farmer network groups and the university: A case study of Missouri's Green Hills Farm project." The research reported here is part of a collaborative study of rural churches in Missouri.

Penny Edgell Becker is a professor of sociology at Cornell University and received her doctorate from the University of Chicago in 1995. She has written extensively on religion and moral culture. Her recent book, *Congregations in conflict: Cultural models of local religious life* (Cambridge, 1999), received the ASA Religion Section Best Book Award in 2000. Her work has appeared in *Religion and American culture*, *Social problems*, and *Journal of marriage and the family*, and, with Nancy Eiesland, she co-edited *Contemporary American religion: An ethnographic reader* (AltaMira 1997). Her current research is on the changing institutional links between religion and family after a period of rapid social change.

Joy Charlton is professor of sociology and associate dean for academic affairs at Swarthmore College. She has broad research interests in gender, work and religion, and in methods of observation and interviewing. She has in the course of her career directed those methods toward better understanding clergywomen, mathematicians, office workers, shiftworkers and their families, back to clergywomen, and, concurrently, though in a somewhat different way, those who live and work in small liberal arts colleges.

Lynn Davidman is associate professor of American civilization and Judaic studies at Brown University. Her past works include the award-winning *Tradition in a rootless world* (University of California Press, 1991) and *Motherloss* (University of California Press, 2000). She has received grants to study women and religion and has published articles in this field, as well as on contemporary ethnographic methods. Her current project is on lived Judaism in everyday life.

Ann M. Detwiler-Breidenbach is a doctoral student in rural sociology and women studies at the University of Missouri-Columbia. Along with the sociology of religion, her research interests include immigration, NGOs, and women, especially at the intersection of the local and the global. She continues to do ethnographic research on the rural church's response to the Hispanic immigration in Missouri as part of the Missouri Rural Church Study. She also collaborates on research studying the role of spirituality in the doctor-patient relationship in the medical setting and works as a mental health counselor at a community health center.

Tanice G. Foltz is an associate professor of sociology and director of women's studies at Indiana University Northwest, where she has taught since 1989.Tanice received her BA at Indiana University at Fort Wayne, a master's in sociology at Arizona State University, and her doctorate in sociology from the University of California at San Diego, where she specialized in qualitative research methods, the new religions, and medical sociology with an emphasis on alternative healing. After graduating in 1985, she taught at several campuses in the California State University system, and co-conducted team research on a feminist witches' coven. After relocating to the Midwest in 1989, she continued her study of Goddess spirituality and uncovered its relation to healing the self, relationships, and addictions. She is the author of *Kahuna healer: Learning to see with Ki* (Garland, 1994). Today she is researching the rapidly growing phenomena of drumming and its connection to healing and the creation of spiritual community.

Zoey A. Heyer-Gray is a graduate student in the department of sociology at the University of Missouri-Columbia. Currently her research interests are focused on the work women do outside of the home and the workplace.

Janet Liebman Jacobs is professor of women's studies at the University of Colorado in Boulder. She is author of *Divine disenchantment: Deconverting from new religions* (Indiana University Press 1989), *Victimized daughters: Incest and the development of the female self* (Routledge 1994) and *Ritual and remembrance: Crypto-Jewish heritage and the recovery of hidden ancestry* (University of California Press, forthcoming). She is co-editor of *Religion, society and psychoanalysis* (Westbiew Press 1997) and *William James: The struggle for life* (SSSR Monograph Series). Jacobs' articles have appeared in *Signs: A journal of women in culture and society*; *Journal for the scientific study of religion*; and *Sociological analysis*.

Adair T. Lummis is faculty associate for research at Hartford Seminary's Institute for Religion Research. She has presented numerous papers and held positions in four professional associations. Since receiving her Ph.D. (Sociology, Columbia University) she has specialized in research on religious organizations, their constituencies and the issues they face. She has coauthored various books over the last twenty years, including: *Women of the cloth: A new opportunity for churches* (1983); *Islamic values in American life* (1987); *Defecting in place: Women claiming responsibility for their own spiritual lives* (1994) ; *Healthy clergy, wounded healers: Their families and their ministries* (1997), and *Clergy women: An uphill calling* (1998). Currently she is studying the role of regional judicatory offices in Protestant denominations in trying to meet competing demands of their congregations and national church bodies.

Nancy Nason-Clark is a professor of sociology at the University of New Brunswick in Fredericton, Canada and coordinator of the Religion and Violence Research Team of the Muriel McQueen Fergusson Centre for Family Violence Research. She received her Ph.D. from the London School of Economics and Political Science in England. Nancy is the author of *The battered wife* (Westminster John Knox Press, 1997) and *No place for abuse* (with Catherine Clark Kroeger, InterVarsity Press, 2001), as well as numerous journal articles and chapters in scholarly books. She is editor of *Sociology of religion: A quarterly review*. Nancy's research program examines the relationship between gender, faith, and culture, and she is currently completing a book tentatively titled *Congregations and family crisis*.

Paula D. Nesbitt is director of the Carl M. Williams Institute for Ethics and Values and on the women's studies faculty at the University of Denver. She is ordained as an Episcopal priest and assists at an inner city parish in Denver. She holds a Ph.D. in sociology and a Master of Divinity from Harvard University. She is author of *Feminization of the clergy in America: Occupational and the organizational perspectives* (Oxford University Press, 1997), a coauthor of *In praise of congregations* (Cowley,1999), editor of *Religion and social policy* (AltaMira, forthcoming 2001), and has published numerous articles on gender and the clergy. Related research interests include the relationship of gender and sexual practice to religion in cross-cultural contexts.

Mary Jo Neitz is a professor of sociology and women studies at the University of Missouri in Columbia, Missouri. She is the author of *Charisma and community: A study of religious commitment within the charismatic renewal*, and, with John Hall, of *Sociology of culture*. With Marion S. Goldman, she is the editor of *Sex, lies and sanctity: Religion and deviance*, Vol. 5 of the series *Religion and the moral order*. She received her Ph.D. from the University of Chicago in 1981. She is currently working on a book on contemporary neopagans and feminist witches.

Lenora Sleep received her MA and BA from the University of New Brunswick in Canada. The chapter she wrote for this edited collection is based upon her thesis, "Women, work and worship: The relationship between the Pentecostal family and modernity." Lenora has written and presented several papers at conferences and has worked as a research assistant for the Religion and Violence Research Team of the Muriel McQueen Fergusson Centre for Family Violence Research.

Michelle Spencer-Arsenault is a Ph.D. student at the University of Waterloo in Canada and received her BA and MA from the University of New Brunswick. Her contribution in this volume is based on her MA research, "Mary, Mary quite submissive: An analysis of Catholic teaching in the lives of practising Catholic women." Michelle has written and presented several papers for both the Society for the Scientific Study of Religion and Association for the Sociology of Religion and contributed book reviews for *Sociology of religion: A quarterly review*. She is particularly interested in how religious teaching helps shape women's lives and identities, and is reconstructed to better fit their modern realities.